Siskiyou County Schools Library
Yreka, California

Last Names First

Last Names First
. . . And Some First Names Too

by
Lee, Mary Price
and
Lee, Richard S.

Illustrated by Weber, Debora

The Westminster Press
Philadelphia

Book design by Christine Schueler

First edition

Published by The Westminster Press®
Philadelphia, Pennsylvania

PRINTED IN THE UNITED STATES OF AMERICA
2   4   6   8   9   7   5   3   1

Library of Congress Cataloging in Publication Data

Lee, Mary Price.
  Last names first.

  Bibliography: p.
  Includes index.
  SUMMARY: Discusses various kinds of personal names such as nicknames and names after marriage and describes how names changed as they traveled overseas and were passed down through generations. Includes a dictionary of common last names and their meanings.
  1. Names, Personal—Juvenile literature. 2. Names, Personal—United States—Juvenile literature. [1. Names, Personal] I. Lee, Richard S. (Richard Sandoval), 1927–   . II. Debora Weber, ill. III. Title.
CS2309.L368 1985   929.4   84-20860
ISBN 0-664-32719-2

To the
Carrs, Dunnings, Keyes, and Pauls,
Very special families

Contents

Introduction:
If Names Could Tell

What stories names could tell if they could talk! Names could complain that they have been shortened, changed, misspelled, and mispronounced. Names could brag that they have launched kingdoms, discovered continents, founded colleges. The name that you so casually sign to a paper may be heir to a very interesting story.

This book may tell you something you didn't know about your own name. It will also give you lots of information about many other names. You will learn all about nicknames, popular first names, names in our computer age, and much more.

For instance, did you know that:
- You could have four last names?
- Your family receives three times as much mail since the development of the computer?
- There's a Mr. A, a Mr. Z, and at least one person with each letter of the alphabet for a last name?

That's only the beginning of name facts.

Let's begin with last names first.

Part One

Last Names First

1 *Your Last Name: Person, Place, or Thing?*

Maybe you've played the guessing game Person, Place, or Thing? This same game can be played with many last names. Your family's last name may be based on a person (from a first name or a nickname), a place (town, field, brook, or castle), or a thing (an object that someone made, or the trade involved in making it).

These three origins account for most of the names from many European countries. Since the majority of such names are found in English, and since English history is the easiest for North Americans to use in tracing where last names came from, most of the examples in this chapter are based on English. But some of the names we see every day come from France, Spain, Italy, Holland, or Scandinavia. These names, and also some Oriental names, generally fit into a person-place-or-thing category, so you will see some examples of these names too.

In ancient Greece, each person had only one name. Aristotle, Socrates, and Plato had no other names. But later, aristocratic Romans usually had three names, as we do: the emperor we know as Julius Caesar was really Gaius Julius Caesar. *Gaius* was similar to Robert or John, a first name. *Julius* identified his clan or tribe and was a name he shared with relatives, while *Caesar* was like our family names and was handed down from one generation to the next.

Some Roman nobles had as many as thirty names, but

13

multiple naming disappeared after the fall of the Roman Empire for the nearly one thousand years of the Dark Ages.

Naming customs were—and are—different in many lands. In some African tribes, boys change their names when they grow up. In others, a father may take another name when his first child is born. Names may be changed when people become ill or grow old. To this day, some Balinese and Turks do not have family names. And there were American Indian tribes that changed members' names to suit the season!

How did we develop last names? The custom reappeared with tenth-century nobles in Venice, followed by the French, Irish, and others, but came most directly from the Anglo-Saxons of the Middle Ages. This is interesting, because originally these people had no family names.

Before Duke William of Normandy sailed from France to conquer England in 1066, the Anglo-Saxons did not have last names—also called *surnames,* from Old French *sur* meaning over and *nom* meaning name. Instead, they used single names, and these worked quite well, because every person's name was different on purpose. When it came time to name a baby, the parents would pick a name they thought no one had ever had. That way, the new baby could not possibly be confused with anyone else. To make sure the name was acceptable, the parents would query the whole family about it. Older family members would be asked if they could remember an ancestor who had used it. If there had once been an Aethelred, for instance, this name would be discarded and the parents would invent another. Of course, no one else in the village where the family lived would have the new name either.

No doubt some names were duplicated in other parts of England, but this was not a problem, because people rarely traveled from the place where they were born, and they almost never moved. There were not too many chances that one Aethelsweord would ever meet another. (*Aethelsweord* in Old English means Noble Sword or

14

Noble Swordsman—a name, like many others of the time, designed to inspire the child to live up to it.)

This system produced a bewildering assortment of names, each supposedly used just once, so none of them have come down to us as family names like your last name today. For this reason, it is almost impossible for anyone to trace family roots to single-name days, or before the year 1300.

When every family struggled to provide its own food and shelter and did little else, the single name was all a person needed to set himself or herself apart from the few people living nearby. The Norman invasion of 1066 changed all that, but the change was gradual. It took nearly three hundred years for everyone to have a family, or last, name. Just to make sure everyone did, King Edward decreed, in the mid-fifteenth century, that every Briton had to have a last name.

Sometimes it took several generations for a particular last name to stick with a family. Since, as we shall see, their names were given to them, not chosen by them, people often changed last names, or were given other ones, in later generations.

In a few years, Duke William of Normandy—by then, of course, King William—brought all England under his control. He divided the country into shires, which remain today: Wiltshire, Hampshire, Devonshire, and so on. To govern each shire he appointed, as earl, one of his Norman followers. The earls, in turn, divided their shires into smaller units called manors. Each manor was ruled by a lord, from which comes the expression "lord of the manor." A very few earls and lords were Saxons who had pledged allegiance to the king. In return for their loyalty, they, like their Norman counterparts, were given absolute power over the Anglo-Saxon peasants in their shires and manors.

Last names were used in France, so it was only logical for the Normans to bring the idea to England. King William had a last name, a place name, "of Normandy," which set him off from any other Guillaume or William. His Norman earls and lords used last names too, and these were often the names of castles or towns they had come from in France; thus we have Robert de (of) Sackville and John de Montague. Later, the French place names were written in English from the French pronunciations; Sinclair comes from St. Clair and Sidney from St. Denis. The few Saxon nobles adopted last names, usually from the English manors they ruled, to show that they too stood well with the king.

Soon after the conquest, King William realized he had taken over a country that was poor indeed compared to France. Every peasant had only the barest necessities for life. There was almost no exchange of goods and services— not even the simplest form of what we would call an economy. The few Anglo-Saxon craftsmen were less skilled than those in France. So King William did the only thing he could—he imported great numbers of Norman craftsmen. Soon, skilled weavers, blacksmiths, potters, and woodworkers were changing the face of England: setting up shops in the villages to provide things the farmers needed in exchange for food. As this was happening, the king made the first real move toward the creation of family names—he took a census. Not until some eight hundred years later in America did anyone else undertake such a giant project. The record he created is called the Domesday Book, and parts of it still exist. It came about in this way.

Twenty years after the conquest, William needed to know the value of the real estate he had given his loyal followers. To find out, and to collect the taxes he felt he deserved in exchange for his generosity, he assembled a group of people who could read and write, no easy task in those days. These traveling clerks recorded the taxable value of the properties they visited and noted the names, mostly of Norman places, of the noble landholders. French names like Neuville (new town) became Neville or Newton. Beauchamp (pretty field) eventually became Beecham or Beacham. When the Domesday Book was

completed, the nobles had their last names on record, but it would be some time before people of lower rank were all given family names.

While the king was busy taxing the nobles, they in turn taxed the farmers and craftsmen in their domains. By this time, many ordinary people had taken simpler names like William (to honor the king), John, Robert, Edmund, Walter, and Andrew. Now, instead of three peasants in a village, all with unique Anglo-Saxon names, there might be three Williams. How could they be told apart so each could be given credit for his taxes? The tax collector gave them last names, person-place-or-thing names.

Person names came about because it was easy to identify a man as "John's son" in the village. Repeated often enough, the name stuck and became the family name. In time, the apostrophe in John's son disappeared, and the two words were combined; the -son ending was often dropped. Since no two tax collectors spelled things alike (and no one could spell very well!), there are today many

variations of the Johnson name, among them Johnston, Johnstone, Jonson, Johns, and Jones. John must have been a very popular first name in early days, because Johnson, with its many variations, is the most common last name in modern America. "William's son," also popular, is of course the literal meaning of today's Williamson, Williams, Wilson, Willis, Wills, and many other family names beginning with Wil. Robertson and Roberts came to us the same way. How many -*son* names can you think of?

Pointing to a man and saying, "That's William's son" was one way of creating a "person" last name. Another was to point to someone and laugh. Suppose the victim was a poor farmer with a stony (*stan* means stone in Old English) field (lea) that was hard to cultivate. Nicknaming him Stony Field (Stan Lea) might, after the joking stopped, become the family name Stanley. Other nickname family names came from physical characteristics such as Swift for the energetic, Ambler for the slow moving, Stout for the fat.

Such nicknames are found in many languages. Brown identifies a person by hair color or complexion. The name would be Bruno in Italian, Marros in Greek, Dun or Dunne in Irish, LeBrun in French, Braun or Brun in German.

Person names like King, Duke, Lord, Prince, Earl, and Queen did not descend from royalty, much as their holders today might like to believe, but are thought to have come from the players in Medieval pageants who took royal or noble parts. Giving these jugglers, minstrels, actors, and dancers royal names was a form of nicknaming.

Far more common than person names were place names. When the tax collector visited the farmers, he might give each a last name that identified him by his surroundings. The farmer with a cottage near a stream might be named Bywater, Brooke, Broke, Brook, or Brooks, depending on the tax collector's spelling ability. If the farmer lived just outside the castle gate, his name might be Atgate (from *atten* and gate), Agate, Gates, or Gatesby. The name Nye comes from *atten eye*, at or on the island. The names Bywood, Byfield, Atlea, Attlee, Appleby, and even our friend Stanley just about explain their own origins. Of the hundred thousand or more English family names, almost half describe where people lived.

Many place names are English spellings of Norman-French words. Boyce, for instance, comes from *bois*, or woods. So Mr. Boyce and Mr. Wood were both peasant farmers who lived in or near woodland. The name each one received depended on whether the tax collector wrote it in French or in Anglo-Saxon.

Place naming, like the other types, occurred in many countries. Hook, Hoke, and Hooker all refer to hook-shaped pieces of land where people lived. Van (of) Hock and Hoekstra mean the same in Dutch; the name in German is Engel (literally, angle) or Hormann. Hill and Hillman are self-explanatory names in English. Germans who lived on hills were named Buehler or Knorr. This very popular name has an equivalent in almost every European language.

Thing names, which came from what people made or did to earn a living, are the most interesting English family names of all. King William's many craftsmen and their descendants helped create a wealth of names during the naming period, 1086 to about 1300. Each occupation brought about many names for the same thing. A potter, for instance, might be so named by one tax collector, or be called Thrower by another, because clay is thrown or turned on a potter's wheel. He could be named Bowler, Bowles, or Boles if bowls were what the tax man saw in his shop. If instead of bowls he made crocks, his name might become Crockard or Crocker. If his pots were little ones, his name might become Potkin or Potkins, since -kin and -kins were word endings that indicated smallness. Someone whose father was a potter might be named Potterson, combining person and thing in one name.

Most occupational names were given to the male member of the household, but a few were awarded to the wives if they were the ones who did the work. The name ending -ster sets the women's names apart. Taper or Tapper is from the Anglo-Saxon *tappere,* meaning a plug for a barrel, removed to let the liquid run out and then replaced to stop its flow. So a Tapper got his name from his job of dispensing ale at an inn. If his wife was the one who tapped the barrel, her family name—and his—might be Tapster. The best-known -ster name is Baxter, originally Bakester, a female baker. Some one named Thaxter is descended from a female thatcher, whose job was making roofs of straw.

Almost every occupation lent itself to names that have survived today. Hall, a very popular name, came from the person in charge of the great hall of a castle or manor house—an important job, since he kept the food and wine flowing and made sure the earl's or lord's guests were well treated. Many place and occupational names included the ending -man, as does Inman, the man who operated an inn.

Of the occupational names that have come to us unchanged, an unusual one is Jester, the fool or clown whose job it was to entertain the king, earl, or lord and his castle or manor-house guests. Another odd name, only slightly changed by time, is Kellogg—a person who killed hogs!

Some names that were famous in later generations came from less-than-aristocratic occupations. Calvert, the family name of Lord Baltimore, means calf-herd or calf-herder.

Many occupational names such as Miller, Baker, Carpenter, Brewer, Sawyer, Clark (meaning clerk), Hunter, Farmer, Cook, Mason, Teacher, and Steward have come down to us without change and with the same meanings they had in the late Middle Ages. But many such names had more than one form, since they could be based on either Norman-French or Middle English words. Butler and Burle are the same name, Butler from *butelier*, Norman-French for someone in charge of wines. Burle, Burls, or Burles is from *byrele*, Old English for cupboard; thus, a person in charge of food and drink.

Fermer was a spelling variation of farmer, but it also meant tax collector, from the Norman-French word *fermier*, freely translated, to catch. One of the many English names for tax collector was Catcher! *Hoff* and *Hoffman* mean farmer in German. *Stad* means farm in Norwegian, so the name Bjornstat comes from the family living for several generations on Bjorn's farm. This is an interesting combination of person and place with the thing (farming) simplified, all in one name.

You probably know someone named Smith. This word comes from the Anglo-Saxon and means one who smites or strikes something. That's exactly what smiths did, and what a few still do today. A smith heated metal over a charcoal fire and then formed it into hoes, knives, swords, or pieces of armor by placing it on an anvil and striking it with a heavy hammer to shape it.

There were so many smiths in England during the naming period that the tax people often had to name individuals after their specialty, to set them apart from other smiths working nearby. Arsnell, Horsnell, Shoesmith, Shouger, and many more are all names for smiths who made horseshoes. Ferrer and Farrier, as well as

Marshall *(maréchal)*, mean the same in Norman-French. A Naylor made nails. Nasmith, Naismith, and Nesmith all specialized in making knives. You don't have to guess what an Arrowsmith and a Hammersmith made.

The smith had assistants, and these too were given names based on the work they performed. Smiths used charcoal for heating, and the many names for charcoal makers include Cole, Coles, Coleman, Collier, and Collyer. And the man who pumped air into the charcoal fire might be named Belloe, Bellows, or Blower.

Almost every occupation lent itself to names that survive today. Chancellor, Dean, Proctor or Procter, Fellows, and Masters are still titles used for university administrators and teachers. Even dog trainers got in on the naming action. Berner or Bernier is Norman-French for a hunting-dog trainer and kennel keeper. Berner, Brackner, and Brenner are the English forms. Entertainer David Brenner might be able to trace his ancestry to one John le Brenner in 1280!

Many Japanese family names came from nature and are thus place names. These names often combine two words in one. Former U.S. Senator and college president S. I. Hayakawa, for instance, has a last name using words for early and river. His ancestors may have lived near a brook or stream, or by the beginnings of a river. Former Japanese Premier Tanaka's name means rice field and middle.

China has the largest population of any country in the world, yet the Chinese share only about a thousand surnames. That's why one sees the same Chinese names over and over: Wong, Lee, Chang, and Ho, for example. Almost always, these are one-syllable surnames. Last names are so important to the Chinese that they are placed first. Wong Chin Yee is not Mr. Yee but Mr. Wong.

The Chinese last name may be simple, but rules of address can be tricky. The American press referred to Dr. Hu Shih, a former Chinese ambassador to this country, as Dr. Shih. But the family name or surname was Hu. However, the Ambassador didn't tell the press that Hu was his surname—so he remained Dr. Shih to the American public.

All Chinese with the same last name are considered members of the same family, even if their ancestral connections cannot be accurately traced. The Chinese have brought their great sense of family to America. In the Chinese communities of most larger American cities, there are benevolent associations operated by Chinese family members and designed to help the same-name members of their families.

Scandinavians, especially those from Sweden, used to have a name system that combined first and last names in succeeding generations, which often confused non-Scandinavians. This confusion sometimes brought about name changes when these people arrived in America.

The next chapter tells something of how last names came to the United States, and Chapter 3 explains how and why some Scandinavians, along with many other peoples, changed their last names along with their nationalities when they reached the new continent.

2 *Last Names Cross the Oceans*

How many different last names are there in North America? The best estimate is 1,250,000! They represent the descendants of people who came from virtually every country in the world as well as those who are still coming.

America grew in much the way a building does—brick by brick, layer by layer. Although people have arrived from everywhere throughout the history of the United States, there were several great waves or "layers" of arrivals from certain countries at certain times.

After Columbus, people from Spain—and from France, too—continued to cross the Atlantic to America, but their interest in this undeveloped land was fleeting. Had they been as eager to settle here as they were to find gold or trap animals for their fur, North America might well have been an extension of central Europe. Instead, it was "Britannized"—settled by the English, Scottish, Irish, and Welsh who dared to cross the seas and colonize the unknown lands.

In the next hundred years, Germans, Scandinavians, and those of other nationalities were drawn to the fresh opportunities offered by America. Often they sent money so relatives at home could join them, thus building up ethnic communities.

Africans, too, arrived on American soil, but by the force of slavery rather than by choice. Their numbers swelled from 59,000 in 1714 to 263,000 by 1754, with more to come, as slave traders plied the oceans.

Blacks have felt rootless from their first unwilling steps upon American soil. Having lived for generations with names forced upon them by slaveowners after their arrival from Africa, many are now choosing both first names and last ones that reflect pride in their African heritage.

The 1800s witnessed continued immigration from Western and Northern Europe. Even when the Civil War was raging, 91,000 people arrived annually! Large numbers sought relief from overcrowded cities and from the loss of family acreage.

Newcomers from other countries were added to the already growing international mix that was early North America. Eastern and Southern Europeans—such as Poles, Czechs, Slovaks, and Italians—headed for U.S. shores as the tide of British immigration slowed.

From 1905 to 1914, immigrants swelled the population by over 10 million. One fifth of these were Italians; other large numbers represented Eastern and Southern European countries. For most new arrivals, their first steps on American soil were across the well-worn floors of the Ellis Island immigration station in New York City.

After 1914, the government placed limitations on the numbers and nationalities of eager would-be immigrants. But the door remained open to tremendous numbers despite the restrictions. Refugees both European and Oriental sought and received entry to America. These displaced people were the fallout of several wars, including recent international conflicts. Others qualifying under the Immigration and Naturalization Act of 1952, amended as recently as 1978, include Canadians, Mexicans, Central Americans, and people from the West Indies and other Caribbean islands.

The English names of those who settled Jamestown, Plymouth, and other colonies pepper the pages of today's telephone books. Smiths, Bakers, Booths, Johnsons, and

Joneses now live everywhere in the United States and have for generations.

Although the colonies were mainly a transplanted United Kingdom, there were also the French—especially in what is now Louisiana, part of a territory originally owned by France—the Dutch in New York, some free Blacks, and a few Italians and others. So the North American melting pot was becoming a reality long before the massive European immigrations of later years.

The young colonies along the East Coast grew and prospered, introducing new names into the American name stream as later immigrants arrived. Early records include such occasional oddities as the Peck brothers. Peck means peak or painted hill, an interesting English surname for two men from the flatlands of southwest England. The Peck ancestors must have traveled from their hilly countryside long before the brothers traveled in turn to the colonies!

Censuses are a treasure trove for *onomasticians* (name experts). The census of 1790 showed America to be predominantly English, featuring all the popular surnames. Smith was a leading name in 1790. Davis, Jones, and Williams also appeared often on census rolls, along with their name variations and spelling changes. The English, almost 80 percent of the American population in 1790, continued to emigrate to America throughout the 1800s, carrying with them the lightweight baggage of their names as well as their lifetime possessions.

Many of the settlers from the British Isles were Welsh. Large numbers emigrated to get away from their overbearing English neighbors, only to find them firmly rooted in America! But they came anyway, bringing names like Price (ap Rhys, meaning son of Rhys), Jones, Evans, Davis, and other surnames hardly distinguishable from English ones.

One famous Welshman, the late actor Richard Burton, whose real name was Jenkins but whose legally adopted stage name means one from a fortified manor, spent much of his time in the United States, although he was not a citizen. But few Welsh are drawn to America today, only those responding to the tug of family ties or professional opportunities.

The Scots emigrated to the American colonies, often by the villageful. Ulster Scots, as they were called, who had been transplanted to Ireland's northwest corner of Ulster by King James I, voyaged to America in search of a more tranquil life. English and Irish neighbors often made life difficult for these sandwiched-in citizens. By the time of the American Revolution, a quarter million Ulster Scots had helped settle the East Coast from New England to South Carolina.

Scots from Scotland came somewhat later and in impressive numbers. More businessmen than toilers of the land, they revered hard work and a good education. They brought with them surnames like Duncan, MacDonald, Maclay, Macleod, Stewart, and Campbell. Other Scottish names are indistinguishable from the British—Smith, Grant, and Wilson, for example.

The Scots in America favored the British during the American Revolution, but their at-home neighbors, the Irish, rallied to the Colonial side.

It was not until the middle of the nineteenth century that the Irish came to the United States in force. Large numbers fled the Irish potato famine and almost certain starvation at home. Kellys and Murphys, O'Briens and Callahans, O'Shaughnessys, Mulligans, and Fitzgeralds boosted the U.S. population and lent their skills and backs to such diverse fields as politics, building construction, and farming. Most of these and other Irish names are patronymics, from the Latin word *pater*, father. O', as in O'Connor, means of or descendant of. Foley is a patronymic meaning grandson of a plunderer. It was originally spelled Foghlaidh.

Although most of the Irish fled from famine, citizens of the various German principalities generally left their countries to escape religious persecution. Englishman William Penn, that openhearted Quaker, offered the Mennonites, a

German religious sect, a large segment of land in Pennsylvania and the chance for peaceful settlement. Most of the people living in today's so-called Pennsylvania Dutch country are the Mennonite and Amish descendants of those early German (*Deutsch*) settlers; relatively few came here from Holland, despite the "Dutch" part of the name.

Other Germans fleeing religious tyranny set a compass course for American shores. By 1790, over 250,000 Germans called the young country their home. Some had fought with the Loyalists or the English; an equal number sided with the colonists.

The Germans who came then and later were hard workers. They approached each challenge—whether farming, furniture making, or metalworking—with industry and skill. That may be why many of their names describe occupations: Schuster means shoemaker; Spangler means tinsmith; and Muller, a miller or grinder of grain.

Other German names reflect appearance or virtue. Some even translate into two word meanings. Gebhart, for instance, comes from *geb,* gift, and *hart,* brave.

Gerhard King Wille, of Bryn Athyn, Pennsylvania, needs to go back only two generations to find his foreign roots. His grandfather, also Gerhard Wille, was a German brickmason who came to America in 1906. He settled in Chicago, in a German community, and continued his trade.

Germans continued to emigrate to America in this century. Many German Jews fled a country gone mad under Adolf Hitler. Albert Einstein was one of them, bringing to America new and startling scientific ideas. His name means builder or stonemason, and indeed he was a builder; his theories in physics and mathematics rebuilt and developed scientific thought worldwide.

Certain segments of the new land were vigorously settled by the Dutch. New York was first called Nieuw Amsterdam, and even in the late 1700s, Albany, New York, was virtually a tiny Netherlands. Two hundred years later, Michigan became home to many Dutch immigrants.

The Dutch brought long and interesting names with

them. Lots of Van (from) and Vander (from the) names crossed the seas—for example, VanSant and Vanderveer. (The German equivalent of Van is Von.) The most famous Van of all was the fictional sleepyhead, Rip Van Winkle. Rip's inventor could choose from two original name sources, from-the-town-of-Winkle or from-a-small-shop. Other Dutch names common in America are DeJonghe, Stuyvesant, Roosevelt, and Roggenfelder, later Americanized to Rockefeller.

America's Scandinavian population was small and scattered until the middle of the nineteenth century. Then, suddenly, American shores were inundated with Petersons, Larsons, Ekholms, Andersons, and Hansens. The Scandinavian countries had dropped their ban on emigration, and Danes, Finns, Swedes, and Norwegians were among those who rushed to claim the 160 acres of land that the U.S. Government was giving to each homesteader. Most of these hardy immigrants settled in the chillier parts of the young country, favoring areas with temperatures most like their own crisp climates.

Spanish-speaking peoples sought the sun of southern, southwestern, and western parts of the country rather than the snowy climes. They were used to countries where 40 degrees could be considered cold! Today, though, they gravitate to many northern population centers, where the Spanish-speaking population is growing faster than any other ethnic group. Even now, Spanish names are crowding out some English ones in the survey of America's fifty most common names.

There was no dramatic head start to account for the Spaniards' generous portion of the population pie in U.S. society today. In early times, the Spaniards came only to seize what treasures they could for home markets; then it was back to Spain to share the booty. That's why Plymouth, not St. Augustine, was the first permanent settlement in the New World.

Eventually, Spaniards came to America in significant numbers. But they did it in a roundabout way. In 1519, for

example, Hernando Cortez, along with such trusty companions as Sandoval, left Spain to conquer parts of Mexico, where many of his soldiers, along with Spanish missionaries, stayed and settled. Subsequently, many of the descendants of Spanish-Mexican unions came to America.

Sandoval, incidentally, was the great-great-great-grandfather of co-author Richard Lee. Mr. Lee's mother, Eunice Celeste Sandoval, was one of those Spanish Mexicans whose family came to America early in the twentieth century. Her ancestry spanned centuries and continents.

Many other Hispanic groups—Cubans, Mexicans, Puerto Ricans, and Filipinos—have come to the United States in recent times. The ancestries of these people are rooted in countries such as Spain and on the continent of Africa, from the Caribbean, and parts of Europe.

Spanish names like Rodriguez, Lopez, Diaz, and Fernandez pop up in school roll calls, in county governments, in parish records. Many of these names belong to people who have distinguished themselves in American expansion. Benjamin Fernandez, for instance, won fame in 1980 as the first Hispanic contender for the U.S. Presidential nomination.

Many Spanish names in America are derived from nature. Blanco and Moreno—white and brown—are descriptive names, for example.

While Spanish populations are growing ever stronger in the United States, French immigration has slowed to less than a thousand a year. Yet at one point North America could have become a New France. Before the American Revolution, our U.S. lineage was in question. But the French and Indian Wars cut the French out of America's future.

History reports that the French did make inroads into the United States via Canada. During the French and Indian Wars, the British drove French-speaking Canadians southward from their Canadian homes. Many settled in what is now the state of Maine, and some moved as far south as Louisiana. Their proud designation is "Cajuns," from their

32

roots in Arcadia, Nova Scotia. Their story is told in Longfellow's poem *Evangeline*.

Other French came not from Canada but from France itself. As Protestants in a largely Catholic country, a minority was forced to look elsewhere for religious tolerance. Calling themselves Huguenots, they left France for America's more open-minded climes. Settling mostly along our East Coast, these were professional people who helped form the backbone of early American society.

Just as Van is almost sure to preface a Dutch name, so a name beginning with Le or Du is most likely French. And again, colors come into the name picture: Leblanc is White, Lenoir is Black. French names, too, are derived from places: du Pont, of the bridge, or from a place with a bridge; du Bois, of the woods; de Villeneuve, of the new town. Other French names include Girard, Roget, and Grenier.

Only in the last hundred years has Italy peppered America with its names. Despite a promising start with explorers Amerigo Vespucci and Christopher Columbus, Italians did not come to the United States in great numbers until the late nineteenth century. This was because Italian emigration was forbidden, just as was Scandinavian.

But after the 1880s, rules were eased and many southern Italians chose to leave their country and seek their fortune across the ocean. Their numbers grew to over 2 million in the first decade of the twentieth century. Many settled in New York, New Jersey, and Chicago, Illinois. The names they brought with them are usually descriptive in nature.

Dr. Rudolfo Rossi of Milan, Italy, arrived recently in Philadelphia. His colorful name means red. Rossi is one of the most popular Italian names in the United States. It is a root name, like Smith for Smithson, Smithfield, Coppersmith, or Smithton. Some famous persons bearing name variations on Rossi are painter Dante Gabriel Rossetti, composer Gioacchino Rossini, model Isabella Rossellini, and singer Julius LaRosa.

Names meaning curly hair, close-cut hair, big head, and

other descriptive characteristics are common. Many show joyousness, like Buongiorno, or good day; Bongiovanni, or good John; de Felice, of happiness; Bontempo, good time; and, of course, Amoroso, love.

Other Italian names frequently heard include Di Giovanni, son of John, and Ferraro, smith, with the newsworthy example, Geraldine.

Accetta means hatchet, although the family coat of arms bears a griffon, a fabled monster symbolic of perseverance and valor. Dintino, another Italian name, means small tooth. A young Dintino might well become a dentist by coincidence, just as we have persons named Doctor who are doctors by profession.

Poles, Czechs, and Slovaks came to the United States from Central Europe. Although their languages and names are somewhat similar, their reasons for coming to America differed. Most Poles emigrated to escape the extreme poverty of their homeland. The Czechoslovaks, on the other hand, first came for political reasons, as war and revolution rolled over their country.

Several Poles fought valiantly in the American Revolution and, later, in the Civil War. But proper recognition of their valor was delayed in at least one case. Vladimir Krzyzanowski, a Union officer in the War Between the States, received his promotion to general belatedly because no one, not even Abraham Lincoln, could pronounce his name!

The Slavs, and this term includes Slovaks, Russians, Yugoslavs, Bulgarians, and Ukrainians as well as Poles and Czechs, were largely country people. Their names are full of good country words: house, chicken, plow, goat, and vineyard. A Yablon, then, in the American telephone book was once a Pole who lived near apple trees. Mr. Kohout, a Czech, had his home near a rooster sign. While Mr. Wishnor may now live in New York City, his Russian forebears were cherry growers. And Mr. Socha, Anywhere, U.S.A., could be Czech, Polish, or Russian. His name means plow in all those languages.

34

Little Hungary has contributed artistic and scientific talent to the United States from its earliest days. But Americans are most familiar with the Hungarians' recent troubles at home. In 1956, many Hungarians participated in a revolt against the Soviet Union. But their courageous efforts were overcome by Soviet military power and many fled the country. Large numbers of refugees came to America, enriching it with their names and talents. Many of their names begin with Sz—Szells, Szucs, and Szonntaghs.

Hungarians Juliesca (Julie) and Tomas Szonntagh of Philadelphia are first-generation Americans. Now in their early twenties and married for several years, they have the best of both worlds—the camaraderie of a large neighboring Hungarian community and the productivity of a rewarding American life. They are proud to be Americans, proud of their Hungarian ancestry, proud to pass on the Szonntagh name to the next generation.

In switching continents to consider Chinese emigration, we also exchange American coasts. Most of the action for the first century of U.S. history was on the eastern seaboard, with English, Dutch, Africans, and others arriving on these shores. But for the Chinese, of course, the western coast of North America was the logical goal.

It was not until gold was discovered in California in 1849 that the Chinese came over in significant numbers. Word of the priceless dust traveled to China as well as to other parts of the world. People of every nationality joined the gold rush for their share of hoped-for fortune. The Chinese were not widely accepted, however, except as low-paid labor.

The early Chinese immigrant generally settled in what was to become the state of California. But eventually, Chinatowns evolved in major cities outside the state, as the Chinese sense of family prompted the immigrants to create their own traditional communities.

The Chinese played a large part in the team effort to build America's first transcontinental railroad. J. N. Hook, author of *Family Names: How Our Surnames Came to*

America, remarks that the job was completed far earlier than it would be today even with our heavy machinery and computers. The industriousness of the many Chinese laborers paid off impressively.

The Vietnamese are among the most recent people to arrive in the United States. In fact, the Vietnamese did not immigrate in large numbers until the mid-1970s. Two hundred thousand of them arrived by sea—many in boats unfit to cross a lake—leaving behind a war-torn country under Communist rule.

Many Vietnamese names sound Chinese, which is not surprising because much of their vocabulary has roots in the Chinese language. Ba, Ky, and Van are typical Vietnamese surnames. An American child with a long last name like McIlhenney might well envy a classmate who has simply to write Ba.

The Japanese, like the Chinese before them, were not always welcome in America. They found, as have many others, that the United States was the Land of the Free only to certain groups at certain times.

The Japanese share outstanding skills in technology with U.S. workers. The two countries cooperate on friendly terms as both American and Japanese cross continents and oceans to work together.

Japanese names go back many centuries. Often these names were chosen for the pleasant sounds they made or because they stood for something meaningful in a person's life.

Japan ruled over Korea from 1894 to the end of World War II. Yet it was not Japan but China that had more influence on the Korean language, probably because of its nearness. Many Koreans have Chinese names as well as their own homegrown names. And again, as with the Chinese and Japanese, the surnames are very short: Yu, Ko, and even K!

Koreans first started coming to the United States in significant numbers after 1910. Many were students fleeing harsh Japanese rule. In the 1950s, there was again an upsurge of Korean immigration. This time, the country was the focus of American and Russian hostilities.

There are certain to be new names as large numbers of immigrants come through America's doors. They will blend with the names that have been brought to the United States from earliest times. New names and new people will continue to reflect the country's strength and diversity.

3 *Last Names Don't Always Last*

Some people who arrived in America years ago decided to trade under their original names. Other names were changed for a variety of reasons.

Because the English settled North America in the greatest numbers, it was only natural that English would become the native language and English names the heritage. But spelling in those years was far from consistent, even among the well educated. Often, names were affected by haphazard spelling. That's why, today, there are many different spellings of last names that sound the same. Kerns is often spelled Kearns or Cairns. Donahue may also be spelled Donohue, Donoghue, Donahoe, even Donahoo. A name like Connelley may have only one l or n or be without the second e. Even a simple name like Lee can be spelled Lea or Leigh.

Europeans often found that Ellis Island immigration officers took liberties with their names. If a name was hard to pronounce, it was probably even harder to spell. So overworked immigration officials often wrote down the name the way it sounded, or close to it—and ever after, the name was spelled (or misspelled) that way. Sometimes, long last names with many complicated syllables were shortened by immigration people—often with the approval of the new American-to-be.

Sometimes even short last names were shortened. President Reagan's great-grandfather was Irishman Michael O'Regan. When O'Regan immigrated to the United States in 1840, the family name was changed to Reagan.

If Lech Walesa, the Polish labor leader, had lived one hundred years ago and come to America, the immigration people might have left Lech alone, or they might have suggested it be Alex instead. But there's a fair chance that Walesa would have been written Vawensa—for that is the way the name is pronounced.

Unless their names were changed for them, most immigrants clung to their original surnames to preserve their identities and keep their cultural backgrounds alive. Many preferred their native languages to English.

Some newly arriving Americans in earlier days did decide to alter their last names. Often, it was the children of these immigrants who felt that a name change was necessary. These changes were sometimes seen by the older generations as insults to family pride and caused resentment. Sometimes only one family member would make a change and the others would defiantly stay with the old name. There were times, too, when the name changers regretted what they had done and returned to their original names.

Many people felt life would be easier for them in the New World with a new name. Stung by the prejudice against their "foreignness," they quickly sought refuge in a simple name. English names like Smith, Carter, and Winslow were easily understood and often adopted by new arrivals. But the so-called Englishness of a name doesn't always make it easy to spell. Take the English name pronounced Chumley. It is spelled Cholmondeley!

Some people simply shortened their names. Chernichenkov might become Chernich, or even Chern. Others selected names that sounded like their old ones, only simpler: Ramsey for Rasmussen, Adams for Adamowicz. Other sound-alikes: Pepper for Pfeiffer, Cook for Koch, Young for Jung, Noble for Knoebel. Among Armenians, a Bedrosian might become Peterson while a Hagopian might prefer Jacobs.

Although some immigrants chose famous American names, name changes also took place within famous families themselves. General George A. Custer, who fought—and lost—the Battle of the Little Big Horn, was descended from a Hessian soldier named Kuester. Kuester was paid to fight for the British during the American Revolution. Pfoersching was the original family name of General John J. Pershing, who commanded the American forces in World War I. And one authority on names says that Abraham Lincoln may have been descended from Germans named Linkhorn.

Sometimes the only connection between the new name and the old one was the beginning letter. Just as buildings may be torn down to the foundations, names lost all but their cornerstone. Balabanoff became Bradley; Walliewicke is now Wells. One man went to court as a Godovsky and left as a Gould.

Some people with supposedly foreign names changed them to their English meanings. This was a good way to preserve one's heritage and adapt to a new country at the same time. Zimmerman means carpenter in German, so there was some logic behind a Zimmerman becoming Carpenter. Schwarz could logically become Black, the literal meaning of the name. Mr. Kurz—even if he was six feet four—could become Mr. Short.

During both world wars, but especially during the first, there were strong anti-German feelings on the part of some Americans. Many Germans hastily abandoned their last names in favor of names that would not invite suspicion. Some of these changes, too, were literal translations—Kaisers became Kings, for instance. Others were not; a Schwermann might choose a sound-alike name like Sherman or become just plain Smith.

The last name appearing on the cover of this book might well be Stopplebein and not Lee if co-author Richard Lee's grandfather had not changed his name during World War I.

41

His name was Joseph Lee Stopplebein, a last name that reflected his Bavarian heritage. He was a brigadier general and commandant of the disciplinary barracks at Fort McPherson, Georgia. Although he had a good sense of humor, he did not like being nicknamed "General Soup and Beans." Finally he dropped his Germanic last name and took his middle name, Lee, as his legal family name. He was not related to General Robert E. Lee. His parents, being Southerners, were admirers of the Confederate general and used his last name as their son's middle name out of respect for Robert E. Lee's leadership. Perhaps the Lee name was more inspiring than General Joseph Lee envisioned. One of his sons and a grandson both became career Army officers.

In most countries, last names usually descend through the fathers of each generation. But in Sweden, at the turn of the century, if a man's name was Lars Carlsson, his son did not have Carlsson as his last name but Larsson: literally,

son of Lars. His father's first name became his last name. Here's how it looked in chart form:

GENERATION	MALE NAME
First	Lars Carlsson
Second	Olaf Larsson
Third	Erik Olafsson
Fourth	Peter Eriksson
Fifth	Edmund Petersson
Sixth	Carl Edmondsson
Seventh	John Carlsson

This custom changed, through the years, to conform to the rest of the world's naming, but many people of Swedish descent today carry names ending in "son."

Oriental names can be written in English only the way

they sound, because written Oriental languages traditionally use pictographs instead of an alphabet. Last names like Chang, Wong, and Lee are written just the way they are spoken.

People usually changed their family names from ethnic to Anglo-Saxon, but there are exceptions. Some years ago, an English actor came to America after a successful stage career as a romantic leading man, the one who always got the girl. His name was Charles Edward Pratt. He became an actor in American movies. One of the first was a horror picture, and Mr. Pratt was given the role of the monster. Then and there, he changed his name. The picture was *Frankenstein*. Charles Pratt's new name was Boris Karloff, and his place in theatrical history was assured by a long list of stage and screen roles, all of which matched his sinister-sounding name.

These days some families with adopted "American" names are changing back to their original family names. Growing family pride and a realization that we are all equal, no matter where our last names come from, are at the heart of these returns to name roots. The son of author Irving Wallace is a writer too. He has reclaimed the family name, Wallechinsky, partly to avoid exploiting his father's career.

While many of today's Americans are keeping their original names, some American Blacks are also returning to their roots by changing to names related to their African ancestry. The ancestors of most black families were brought to America as slaves. They were given English first names by their English, Scottish, or Irish owners, but last names were often not considered necessary. Some slaves did use their African names in the privacy of their homes.

Frank Yerby, in his historical novel *The Dahomean*, describes a black emigrant who was previously an African prince. In the novel, Nyasanu Aguasu Hwesu Gbokau Kesu from the kingdom of Dahomey in West Africa is

44

dubbed Wesley Parks by his white owner. The new name severs old links with the prince's illustrious past and is a daily reminder of his unfortunate situation.

When the slaves were freed in 1865, many found themselves without a last name. Some adopted the last names of their former owners. Others named themselves after people they admired. The two famous Washingtons, George and Booker T., were heroes to a struggling minority. Their surnames were chosen so often that now four fifths of the Washingtons in the United States are Blacks.

Today, many Blacks are attempting to trace their ancestries and are renewing their interest in African history and culture. They are choosing both first and last names that relate to either their origins or their religious beliefs. Retired prizefighter Muhammad Ali long ago changed his name from Cassius Clay. Basketball great Lew Alcindor is now Kareem Abdul-Jabbar. The late Malcolm X, born Malcolm Little, decided upon the Orthodox Islamic El-Hajj Malik El-Shabazz as the name that best fitted his new political stand.

So names, whether adopted or original, play a very important role in one's sense of identity. Last names do indeed come first in the minds of many Americans.

45

4 A Classroom
Pursues Last Names

Everyone has roots, forebears to be traced by playing follow-the-leader in reverse. In this case, the leaders are the oldest living relatives in both parents' families. These people—grandmothers or great-uncles, perhaps—may have old family records or at least recollections that can help you go back in time. They can pinpoint the places your families came from and the ancestors who left their villages or cities for America.

The junior high school students of Germantown Academy, a private school near Philadelphia, did exactly that. They decided to see how much they could find out about their past.

The seventh-graders who set out upon their genealogical tasks may seem very much alike to the outsider. The girls wear uniforms of crisp white blouses and red and blue plaid skirts. The boys are all neatly dressed in shirts, ties, slacks, and blazers.

But appearances are deceiving. These youngsters come from vastly different backgrounds and bring to the school and to their friendships a fascinating diversity. Although most of their parents and grandparents were born in America, their great-grandparents and great-great-grandparents sometimes came from various corners of the world.

Many came from the British Isles; several from Russia,

Poland, Hungary, Lithuania, and Rumania. A few of these U.S. immigrants were from Germany and Austria, some from the Philippines.

When Emily Eastlake asked her maternal grandparents, the MacColls, where their grandparents came from, Mrs. MacColl told her granddaughter that they emigrated from Ulster County, Ireland. Steve Pokorny's four great-grandparents made their trips to America from France, Germany, and Bohemia. Kimberly Bishop found out that her great-grandmother was Helen Elizabeth Peck, a descendant of great-great-great-grandparents who came from England and Ireland.

Several of the students found that they had famous names in their past. Daniel Boone, Aaron Burr, Ulysses S. Grant, and Dolley Madison, wife of President James Madison, numbered among prominent forebears. One student had great-great-grandparents working with famed medical researcher Louis Pasteur; another boasted an illustrious Polish general in her background. And Amy Clemens traced her family back six generations to claim that salty gentleman Samuel Clemens, better known as Mark Twain.

Not too far from Germantown Academy is the Elkins Park School. Sixth-grade students in this suburban school entered a nationwide contest, the History Day—Family Genealogy Competition. Some of the pupils wrote such impressive papers that they were eligible to compete in the state finals.

Marla Dansky was first-place winner with her study "Elka of Warsaw." Marla brought her family up-to-date from life in nineteenth-century Poland to the unthinkable Holocaust of the twentieth century and flight to America. Fellow classmate Heidi Herner discovered the Schwalon family, her Hessian ancestors, a branch of her family tree in seventeenth-century Germany.

Many of the other 63 students participating in the History Day competition found that they were ethnically multilayered—spice in the great American stew.

The Germantown Academy youngsters and the Elkins

Park students found their roots through interviews with relatives. There are other ways to trace your ancestors. Libraries offer genealogy books for young people that give an open sesame to the past.

Here, briefly, are some of the ways to fill out a family tree.

1. Check out old family photo albums, diaries, and pictures.

2. Ask to see birth, baptismal, and confirmation certificates; also marriage certificates.

3. See if your parents, grandparents, or relatives have old wills or deeds that you can study.

4. Explore military records, old ledgers, the family Bible, or scrapbooks.

5. Try to visit the cemeteries where your relatives are buried and check names and dates on gravestones.

6. Ask relatives what organizations (the church, the Elks, the Polish-American Congress, Society of Mayflower Descendants, etc.) your family members belonged to. You will find the national address of these organizations in your local library. Check their membership records and publications.

7. Visit the library. Libraries often have sections on local history. A librarian may be able to give you some useful information from reference material or to suggest other places in the township or county that you should visit.

8. Go to the town or city hall, where there are land and birth and marriage records.

9. Write to state historical societies and archives, where historical information is stored; your librarians will have addresses for these helpful sources. They will also have advice.

10. The U.S. census may tell you about your family:
    Places of birth
    Who was considered head of the household
    Whether the family were naturalized citizens
    How many children and their ages
    Date of parents' marriage

How long the father and mother were in America
Day of their arrival and country of origin
Language spoken by the family
Occupations
Type of home (farmhouse, new house, etc.)

11. Visit or write to the National Archives offices in Boston, Massachusetts; Atlanta, Georgia; Bayonne, New Jersey; Chicago, Illinois; Denver, Colorado; Fort Worth, Texas; Seattle, Washington; San Francisco, California; Los Angeles, California; Philadelphia, Pennsylvania; or Washington, D.C. The National Archives hold U.S. census records of 1790 through those of recent years.

Taken every decade, censuses reveal many, many facts about every single family in the country. After they are taken by thousands of census takers who fan out across the country to collect the information, the censuses are sealed for a period of seventy years: The census statistics are not available to the public for that period of time. The 1910 census is the latest one publicly available. If you can trace your family roots back to 1910, you will be able to find your family's record in the 1910 census archives.

Immigration records for some 10 million American immigrants are now being computerized by the Balch Institute for Ethnic Studies in Philadelphia, from the National Archives' immigration reports filed by ship captains.

Young black people on their way to discovering their roots might well be inspired by Alex Haley, who started many Americans on an ancestor hunt. But Mr. Haley is not the only black person associated with root digging. Mrs. Thelma Doswell of Washington, D.C., spent fourteen years on her genealogical chart. By the mid-seventies she had produced a family tree bearing 3,300 relatives!

Mrs. Doswell, a special education teacher, traced her ancestors back to 1735. In that year, one of her forebears was bought at a slave auction by the Blackwell family of Yorktown, Virginia. This event is the cornerstone of the document. The oil-painted family tree then unfolds to show the eleven subsequent generations.

This unflagging historian discovered that her relatives, both living and dead, represented many groups of people. Africans, Europeans, and American Indians made her family both interracial and international.

The root steps followed by Alex Haley and Thelma Doswell are available at your local library in *Black Genealogy* by Charles L. Blockson and Ron Fry.

Part Two

First Names, Nicknames, and Fame Names

5 *Your First Name and Who Shares It*

Parts of the first three chapters considered the meanings of last names. First names have special meanings too. First names can come from the Bible, as John, the Lord is gracious; from traits, as Valerie, strong, healthy; from achievements, as Robin, of shining fame; from cities and towns, as Devon; and from many other sources.

If you are interested in the meaning of your first name, go to your local library and ask for any how-to-name-the-baby book. You will find the meaning of every name you have ever heard of—and a few you haven't.

If your name is Jennifer, Mary, Karen, Michelle, Jessica, Katherine, Rebecca, Deborah, Robin, or Megan, you share your name with many others. These were the top-ranked girls' names for a recent year. The ten most popular boys' names in the same year were Michael, Jason, Matthew, David, Brian, Christopher, John, James, Jeffrey, and Daniel.

Although these choices are the standout names, there is still great variety in naming. In a recent year in Pennsylvania, for instance, 160,000 children received 12,774 different names. That's a lot of names!

What causes name popularity or name fashions? Why has Barbara, once so popular, been replaced by Jennifer as one of the top ten? Why has Brian won out over a traditional favorite, Richard? With Michelle and Jessica, Jason and

Jeffrey recent name-poll winners, it appears that people are looking for names that will stand out. Perhaps, in a world of increasing imitation—sitcoms, look-alike neighborhoods, TV dinners—parents want names for their children like Anastasia or Everett, that are different from the old favorites.

The 1984 confirmation class of Bruton Parish Episcopal Church, Williamsburg, Virginia, is a good example of recent name trends—a mixture of old and new, formal and informal:

Aaron	Helen	Martin
Alice	James	Mary
Andrew	John	Meredith
(three)	Joseph	Murray
Christopher	Kimberly	Nancy
(four)	Kristine	Robert
Dwayne	Madeline	Sarah
Elizabeth	Margaret	Theresa
Ellen	Maribeth	Zoë

In a 1984 report, the New York Department of Health disclosed many names that were spin-offs of soap operas. Devon, Jenny, and Lisa are all soap inspirations.

One way to be different is to use a nickname as a given name. Many parents use nicknames in middle names as well as first or given names, perhaps because they like their informality. Pearl Betty Stevens of Bridgeton, New Jersey, has a nickname middle name. With two equally attractive names to use, she opted for Pearl, a jewel name.

Jimmy Carter, our 39th President, is another person who uses a nickname as a given name. He marched down Pennsylvania Avenue on his inaugural day with a name meant to make him approachable to all the people.

Do people who decide to remain Jimmy or Billy, Susie or Marcy as adults tend to be different from those who graduate to the more formal names of James, William, Susan, or Marcia? Probably not. But there has been a study on how people feel about formal and informal names. People in business and social activities who face the world with a formal name, like George Dunning, Mary Carr, or Crosby Hoff, tend to be harder workers and more reliable, according to this survey. The Cindys and Stevies on the other hand, have Peter Pan problems in the eyes of others—"they never grew up; they never grew up." They are simply not considered as steady or industrious. The study clearly showed that it was important to use the formal version of a given name to earn the respect of others.

Yet many people who use initials for their names, surely even more abbreviated than nicknames, are perceived as very formal, important people. Initials connote power—for example, J. P. Morgan, financial genius; J. Paul Getty, oil magnate.

People often use one or two initials instead of full names because they don't like their given names. Others get complicated and impressive names because they are bearing the name mantle of some great-great-grandparent.

W. W. Keen Butcher of Philadelphia was named after his maternal grandfather, William Williams Keen Butcher. He, like many others initial-named, is called by various names: Butch, William, and Keen.

Initial names are not always because of family tradition. Boys and girls given double names by their parents—Betty Jo or John Arthur often become "initialed" by their friends. B.J. and J.A. are easy, friendly ways to address pals. Such names are also very distinctive and individual.

There are other name ways to show your individuality. Black parents are now bestowing upon their children African names to give them a sense of their own heritage. Acher Elma Quisro is one of them. Other girls' names are Adamma (Nigerian), child of beauty, and Safiya (Swahili), clear-minded. For boys, Kefentse (Tswaria), conqueror, and Jumah (Muslim), Friday, are popular names.

Here are some other popular names for American children of different nationalities: Kameko (Japanese), child of the tortoise; Setsu (Japanese), fidelity; Shumana (Hopi Indian), rattlesnake girl; Apang (North American Indian), first-place winner. There are the Hebrew popular names, David, Samuel, Ruth, and Sarah. But there are some less common Hebrew names appearing after many centuries. Little girls can be called Jora, autumn rain. Ranon, to be joyous, is a distinctive boy's name.

The names mentioned in this chapter have been distinctly male or female. But there have been some crossovers. Girls are now taking on boys' names—and are proud of them. Jerome, Gary, and Max were on recent birth certificates for Pennsylvania baby girls. Charly is the adopted name of Charlotte McClain, country music singer.

Another well-known singer, Debby Boone, named one of her girl twins Dustin. "I like unusual names for children," says Ms. Boone, wife of Gabriel Ferrer. The other twin is named Gabrielle, after her father.

Finally, Princess Michael of Kent, a lady-in-waiting to England's Queen Elizabeth, apparently finds her masculine name quite acceptable. The princess doubtless has many traditional first names in her illustrious background and could have plucked one from the royal family tree had she wanted to.

Are boys borrowing also? A few parents have chosen a girl's name for their newborn son; the 1982 Pennsylvania male infant roll call included the names Louise, Deborah, Patsy, and Karen. And Keith Richards of the Rolling Stones gave his son a name shared by many girls, Marion.

Crossover names may prove troublesome. Names also have other ways of taking on greater significance than they should. A 1984 survey, taken to determine which women's names men choose from job applications for managerial positions, indicates that names play a strong role in the work world.

Women named Ethel and Myrtle were far more likely to be hired for important jobs than those with first names like Christine or Candace, according to this name survey. Psychologist Deborah Linville of Troy, New York, found

that bearers of no-nonsense names (lined up behind Ethel and Myrtle were Florence, Mildred, Alma, and Edna) were chosen for managerial jobs over those with softer names like Cheryl, Melanie, Dawn, Heather, Jennifer, Marilyn, Michelle, and Susan, as well as Christine and Candace.

Male personnel managers feel that people with popular soft names are less likely to direct others effectively. Those with hard old-fashioned names are, in turn, more successful holding the business reins.

Choosing a woman for a job because of the sound of her name shows unconscious but nonetheless real prejudice, and the survey proves that once again names are emotionally charged.

Researchers at Tulane University have found that girls with first names like Kathy, Christine, or Jennifer are more likely to be thought attractive, and to win beauty contests, than girls with old-fashioned-sounding names. Does this mean that attractive names could help people in business or politics? It is possible. Can you imagine a President named Algernon? Would a woman with a cute name have as good a chance of succeeding in medical school as one with a traditional name like Mary or Sarah? Would Sandra Day O'Connor have been the first woman on the U.S. Supreme Court if she used Sandy?

A nickname from his college days when he played a lightning game of football has not hurt one Supreme Court justice. Byron R. White is still known, among his friends, as Whizzer White.

First names have appeared on everything from bumper stickers to T-shirts. People like to see their names in print. Mail-order houses have capitalized on this, devoting entire catalogs to personalized items. Jill buys a T-shirt proclaiming "I'm Jill" and feels very special until she runs into another young lady whose T-shirt announces "I'm Jill."

Tom is one of the many names that is sewn on a pocket patch, placed on a coffee mug, imprinted on a pencil case. Tom is a very popular name. In fact, there are at least 2 million Thomases around the world. Recently, a small

Welsh town decided to do something for all those Thomases. Tenby, a seaside resort, held a party to lure Christmas holiday shoppers. Assuming that the local population held a goodly number of Thomases, they featured events like Thomas rugby, Thomas sausages, and a 10 percent discount on hotel rates to Thomas registrants. The invitation to Thomases was issued worldwide but an attendance report on the foreign Thomases has not been divulged.

The party director's name was *not* Thomas. It was Ian Bell. But for this occasion fellow committee members dubbed him Bell the Thomas, to fit in with the honored guests.

6　Your Name When You Say "I Do"

Today, when the right man proposes marriage, the answer may be yes, but with a catch. The bride will keep her name, thank you. Name trends mirror the times, and on her wedding day Ms. Swartz may become—Ms. Swartz! Or as a partial concession to tradition, she may hyphenate old and new names to become Ms. Swartz-Jenkins.

Geraldine Ferraro, first woman Vice-Presidential candidate, refers to herself as a married Ms. She has retained her maiden name professionally, but to her social friends, the PTA, and others she is Mrs. John Zaccaro.

Maureen McTeer, wife of former prime minister Joe Clark, of Canada, chose not to combine her name with her husband's. She is Maureen McTeer, wife, mother, and feminist. Her refusal to respect tradition in this instance angered many of her countrymen and a few of her countrywomen. The outspoken McTeer ignored the protests and pursued her causes in her own way with her own name.

Other married women are rethinking their name status. Those who go into law, politics, medicine, and other fields want their accomplishments credited to their own names.

When a major women's magazine recently surveyed its readers on marriage and name changes, the camps were split evenly. A woman should take her husband's name when she marries, said 37 percent; she should keep her own name, responded 36 percent; and 26 percent said, "Try to reach a compromise."

The women who voted to keep their own names were adamant about it. They had fought long and hard for their own bank accounts and credit cards. Surely this investment in time and patience would be lost if they were to give up their names in marriage.

Although opinions differed, those who participated in this survey agreed on one thing: The decision to keep one's name is not just a fad; it's a growing trend, backed by a 70-percent vote of the readership. And this figure includes the most conservative of the magazine's readers. While these traditionalists will not keep their own names when they marry, they see more women heading for their honeymoons with their maiden names on the luggage tags.

What about male decisions and surnames? Rarely does a young man decide he will change his name to that of his fiancée! But here's one exception to tradition: David Camesi of Manhattan Beach, California, became David Champion after he married Janice Champion.

A man who gives up his surname may cause family heartbreak. Names, although invisible, play concrete roles in family relationships. Parents of a newly engaged man wrote advice columnist Ann Landers about their son's decision to take his future wife's name. This controversial step started a family feud. Relatives vowed they would not attend the young man's wedding if he insisted on going through with his plans. Ann Landers sympathized with the disappointed parents and pointed out the obvious reason for this unusual move: The bride's father had no sons to carry on the family name and was pressuring his future son-in-law to take the bride's family name.

Names can also be a war zone for a married couple awaiting the birth of their first child. The woman who insists on keeping her name when she marries may also want her name in the new baby's surname. This is what happened to future parents Lynn Litterine and husband

Marc Kaufman, both of Philadelphia. Ms. Litterine—she did not take her husband's name after marriage—insisted that her name be included with his as the baby's last name. Her husband was very unhappy with the idea. It wasn't fair, he said, to ask a small child to cope with a big name. And besides, he wanted the baby to have his last name, period. The tradition of male name succession was particularly important to him.

But Ms. Litterine insisted on the double last name, vowing she would convert it to a single name if the child was unhappy with it.

The final chapter is that David Litterine-Kaufman, age three, is quite content with his double-jointed last name. In fact, he has plenty of multi-name companions at play-school. Three of his friends sport hyphenated last names.

In spite of Mr. Kaufman's objections, a double last name is really not so cumbersome. Most fit neatly on a signature line of a credit card or passport. Mary Carr-Dunning for instance, does not spill over the dotted line. But supposing Mary Carr-Dunning marries John Hoppe-Buerkle. Is their child going to be John (or Joan) Carr-Dunning-Hoppe-Buerkle? The poor kid will buckle under the weight of such a freight-train name!

Jane Fonda solved the dilemma of last-name confusion. While she remains Jane Fonda and her husband is Tom Hayden (not Mr. Fonda!), their son carries neither of their names. His name is Troy O'Donovan Garity, for reasons not yet divulged by the parents. Troy, of course, may someday want to affix one or both of his famous parents' last names, but in the meantime he has his own identity.

7   Nicknames:
Where Bitsy Is Large

When she was in seventh grade, Bitsy Large was 5 feet 10 inches tall. Her nickname was—and is—a friendly joke; it means just the opposite of what it says. She is now Bitsy Large Carey; her real first name is Emily.

Any big man, last-named Little, is almost automatically going to be nicknamed Tiny whether he likes it or not.

Reverse meaning is only one form of nicknaming. Nicknames of various kinds have been with us throughout history. Among the early ones was Charles the Bald, who was crowned king of France in A.D. 840. How accurate were such unflattering nicknames for ancient kings as Ethelred the Unready of England and Charles the Mad of France? This same Charles was also called the Well-Beloved. Check your history books to see. You'll find that Russia's Ivan the Terrible more than lived up to his less-than-inspiring nickname.

The word nickname is as old as the custom. It comes directly from the Middle English word *nekename* (additional name). During the English naming period, last names like Brown, Black, White, Stout, and perhaps Large were really nicknames, since they described a person's looks. In Medieval days, William Stout and William Small were so-called to set them apart by their appearance rather than by what they did or where they lived.

Other nicknames indicated popularity and prowess. Royalty, especially, wore crowns of praise as well as gold. Duke William of Normandy became King William the Conqueror. King Richard I earned the nickname Coeur de Lion (French), or Lion-Hearted, because of his fearlessness.

Even today, certain nicknames can make their owners feel special. The Rev. Jesse Jackson, activist, minister, and recent Presidential candidate, has five children. Once known as Country Preacher, Jackson nicknamed his second son, Jonathan, Little Country Preacher. Although his oldest boy wanted this title, the privilege went to the second son. Jackson felt that the younger boy, often in the shadow of his older brother, needed something special. The adaptation of his father's onetime nickname filled the bill.

Nicknaming is international as well as historical. In China, with its huge population and small number of last names, many people have identical first and last names. A business corporation in Shenyang City was overpopulated with Li Wei's. The company solved the similar-name confusion among its employees by using nicknames. Several people, all named Li Wei, were set apart with names such as Big, Number 2, Big Eyes, and Long Braids Li Wei.

These are very kind, gentle nicknames compared to some that may be given to people. Carol and Gwynne Gambit of Oak Harbor, Washington, for instance, might resent the nickname of Barbarian Sisters, a reference to their interest in bodybuilding, although the townspeople are proud of them. Their award-winning iron pumping has earned them this colorful nickname.

Although it is not an attractive nickname, Fats probably helped the jazz piano career of Thomas "Fats" Waller. It surely didn't limit the billiards-playing skills of Minnesota Fats, either. This double nickname, of place and appearance, is not common; most people get along with one.

Another double nickname was the one acquired by the late Louis Bert Lindley, Jr., a cowboy in search of a different career. In the 1930s, Lindley became a rodeo clown and broncobuster. He said that, as a living, "It was sure slim pickings." Later, as movie actor Slim Pickens, Lindley built a solid career with work in such films as *One-Eyed Jacks, Dr. Strangelove,* and *Blazing Saddles.*

Single nicknames are often just short informal variations of first or last names. Margaret becomes Marge, Margie, Meg, Margo, Maggie, Peg, Peggy, or just Marg. Richard is Rich, Richie, Rick, Ricky, Dick, or Dickie. William can be Will, Willie, Billy, or Bill. Jonathan is shortened to Jon (note the spelling), while John most often becomes Jack or Johnny. Among last names, Kelly becomes Kel, and many a Peterson is nicknamed Pete.

Nicknames can also be affectionate or even silly. Recent Valentine Day greetings in one metropolitan newspaper produced such funnies as Pasta Bunny, Huggie Bear, Sweet Baboo, Moonah, Booby, Fluffer, Chucky Bird, Nutburger, Boo, Moo, and Puddles.

Pinky might also be appropriate for a Valentine name,

but in this case it belongs—would you believe—to an astronaut who participated in a 1984 space shuttle mission. Pinky, or George Nelson, as he is known more formally, made space history when he retrieved the Solar Maximum Satellite to be repaired in the shuttle's cargo bay. Nelson doesn't think his nickname is unusual. "I've never been called anything else," he commented.

Nelson's fellow astronaut, James "Ox" Van Hoften, has no comment about his nickname, but it could well be that his 6-foot-4-inch frame and athletic physique had something to do with it. Although strong as an ox—he almost played pro baseball—Van Hoften's height proved an obstacle to his ambitions as an astronaut. Imagine a body that size floating in a compact space shuttle! But on a subsequent try for a piece of the sky, Ox Van Hoften was accepted.

Celebrities of another sort sport childhood nicknames. The Travolta kids all had nicknames for each other. John

Travolta's sisters and brothers called him Bone because he was so skinny. Joey was the Head—he had a big head as a little kid. Brother Sammy was Pinch, Margaret was Bobbinhead. And Ellen Travolta had to suffer with Hippo because she was heavy and awkward.

The Travolta nicknames and many others are largely descriptive. Do nicknames reflect the nature of people as well as their appearance? No one can be certain. Some of our Presidents don't take to nicknaming, while others do. Georgie would never do for George Washington, but Abraham Lincoln, General Washington's equal in statesmanship, didn't object to his tag of Honest Abe. President Theodore (Teddy) Roosevelt was never taken too seriously, but his cousin, President Franklin D. Roosevelt, was a serious man for serious times. His initials, FDR, were as close to a nickname as he ever got, and they were given him by the press. The same goes for LBJ: Lyndon, as in President Lyndon B. Johnson, is a nickname-proof first name. On the other hand, Gerald almost too easily becomes Jerry, as it did for President Ford.

There are colorful nicknames aplenty in sports. Dr. J and Wilt the Stilt Chamberlain play basketball. In baseball you can find Yaz, Campy, Tug, always at least one Lefty, and the largest assortment of animal names outside a zoo: Bull, Chicken, Cobra, Goose, Jaybird, Kitty, Loon, and Penguin.

Nicknames aren't universally welcome, as you know if you're stuck with Four-Eyes, Skinny, Stinky, Porky, Slats, Nutsy, or Slug. Barbara and Charles Keyes of Moorestown, New Jersey, purposely gave their children names that were hard to nick: Karen and Brian. Although the Keyes children are now in their twenties, no one has turned their names into Kari and Bri. And more recently, in an effort to zap any would-be nicknamers, former Beatle Ringo Starr named his first child Zak.

8 What If You Don't Like Your Name?

How would you like to be named Humpty Dumpty Jones? In Lewis Carroll's *Through the Looking Glass*, Humpty Dumpty says, "*My* name means the shape I am— and a good handsome shape it is, too." He is content with his odd name, but he thinks Alice is "a stupid name enough."

After all, you didn't choose your own name; your parents presented it to you. Maybe, at the moment, you don't even like it. If it's any consolation, you're not alone. *Parade* magazine revealed in a recent survey of college students that 46 percent were not pleased with their names. The article also noted that the highest proportion of drop-outs from one Ivy League college had unusual first names.

What can you do if you don't like your name? You can change it informally. But before you switch from shrinking Violet to popular Patty or from stodgy Cyril to charismatic Chris, be sure you're basically pleased with yourself. A name change may indeed help your image, but only if your personality has to deal with a name that just doesn't seem to fit.

Dr. Edward Crill, a Harrisburg, Pennsylvania, counselor and name authority, says that names are a matter of iden-tification. If a name, especially a first name, doesn't estab-lish what a person sees as his or her correct identity, unhappiness can result.

Parents often give children names as a way of continuing the family heritage, according to Dr. Crill. Name problems come about with some youngsters if they feel their names are too unique. Others are bothered by having names that are too ordinary.

Not every Tom, Dick, and Harry wants to be Tom, Dick, or Harry. But not every Free wants to be Free, either. This was true of young Free Carradine, son of Barbara Hershey and actor David Carradine. Free changed his odd first name to Tom.

Dr. Crill reports that some parents give their children odd names such as Blaze and Atari to call attention not to their children but to themselves. When Barbara Hershey named Free Carradine, she was using Seagull as her own first name, a double bid for attention.

The story of Busanda Elaine Skevofelix Sciaccitano is typical. She changed her name legally to Sandra Elaine Taggart. Busanda, a name she never liked, came about because her father worked for the U.S. Navy's BUreau of Supplies AND Accounts when she was born. Her Italian last name was hers by a former marriage, and Skevofelix mirrored the strict upbringing of her Greek heritage. Sandra kept Elaine to honor a beloved grandmother and chose Taggart after a respected character in her favorite novel.

Tradition-minded parents sometimes give their children family names as first names. Wharton Sinkler, for example, carries two famous Philadelphia family names into the future, and he's happy to do so. But not every youngster takes kindly to a last name as first name. They feel that a "different" first name like Pendleton or Henderson is heavier to tote than a schoolbag!

Other first-name irritations include names that are old-fashioned, like Patience or Wilfred; names with negative history, like Adolf; girls' names like Josepha (because the parents really wanted a boy); or first names that sound silly with their last names. Examples: Jack B. Quick, Betty Getty, or Willie Gamble.

72

What if your first, middle, and last names produced an unfortunate three-initial combination like P.I.G., D.U.D., F.A.T., D.U.M., or S.L.Y.? Would you change one of your names? Lots of people have.

Other name problems include being confused with someone else and having a name that's hard to spell or pronounce. Patrick MacNee, star of the popular TV show *The Empire,* has both problems in one name. He says he has frequently been taken for British Sergeant McNee of Scotland Yard; McNee was dismissed after an intruder got past Buckingham Palace security guards and into Queen Elizabeth's bedroom. Patrick MacNee has also been confused with a Mr. McBee, and his name has been given numerous misspellings. According to a recent interview, the slipups were annoying. McNee—sorry, MacNee—obviously wishes people would get his name right.

An article in *Seventeen* magazine says that girls tend to change their first names more than boys do. Since their last names will very likely change when they marry, though not always, their first names become very important. Many girls want to have just the right spelling or tone for their first names.

Here are some name-change suggestions.

Girls can vary the first-name spelling. Ellen can become Ellyn or Elli, Betty can change to Bett, Bette, or even Betti; Kathleen to Kathy, Kathie, Kathi, Kate, Katie, or Kati. Jean may be spelled Jeanne or Jeane, or the nicknames Joanie or Jeannie can take over the name job full-time. The opposite often happens, too, especially with childhood nicknames. Babby Lee changed over to her real name, Barbara, during high school and has stayed with it.

Boys can change first names as easily as girls but are less interested in making spelling changes. Let's say your full name is John Douglass Jones, but Johnny Jones simply isn't *you.* You could become J. Douglass Jones, Douglass Jones, Doug Jones, or simply J. D. Jones, with J.D. as your first name.

Using the first two initials instead of a first name is done more in the South and Southwest than elsewhere in the United States, especially for men and boys. Perhaps the custom was encouraged by the infamous J. R. Ewing of *Dallas*. A few girls do it, too. One attractive woman built a successful acting career in part through her two-initial name, K. T. Stevens. In her case, the two initials were memorable and gave her the equivalent of a clearly feminine first name.

If you do decide to use double initials instead of your first name, do yourself a favor and don't drop your first two names legally in favor of the two initials you prefer. Advice columnist Ann Landers received a letter from a man whose parents had legally named him with two initials only. Poor C.E. had constant problems with credit cards and military papers, because people couldn't believe that his initials weren't backed up by first and middle names. C.E.'s letter was not to ask for Miss Landers's advice but to warn parents not to give children initial-only names. When other kids asked for ball gloves and bikes, C.E. said he would have settled for just a regular name, so he could be somebody.

Many men do choose to call themselves by double initials, while retaining their given names for legal purposes. Among them are famous writers. T. S. Eliot, H. G. Wells, D. H. Lawrence, and J. D. Salinger. Even more distinctive was the writer e. e. cummings, who never used capital letters.

Another writer, who is also a concert pianist, changed his name from Paul Harvey, Jr., to Paul Aurandt. He took his own middle name as his last name because he wanted to succeed on his own without capitalizing on the fame of his broadcaster father, Paul Harvey.

Percy Ross, known as the Millionaire and famed for giving money to deserving people, had this name exchange with a couple who said they would name their first baby Percy, in his honor, if it was a boy. Would Mr. Ross start their son off with a $100 bond? "I had a rough time with the name Percy as a boy," Mr. Ross replied. "I wouldn't

recommend it. Whether it's a boy or girl, your baby will get the U.S. Savings Bond."

Here's a final thought for you on name changes. The name you don't like now may appeal to you in a few years. And if you do like your name, even though it is a hand-me-down or a tongue twister, you are probably comfortable with yourself. "Like me, like my name" could be your motto.

9 Celebrity Names People the World

Do ordinary people name their children after celebrities? Indeed they do. It's a custom handed down from the earliest days of naming, as shown by the great popularity of the name William in England after the Norman Conquest engineered by William the Conqueror. And as recently as 1982, Americans were endowing their youngsters with celebrities' names. In Pennsylvania five sets of parents named their boys Elvis. Two Cleopatras and a Napoleon were also recorded among the state's births that same year.

The Bible has been a great source of names, including Abraham, Elisha, and David (but rarely, if ever, Goliath!) among the boys; Martha, Rebecca, and the ever-popular Mary for girls. Today, however, *Jet* magazine reports that first names tend to come from popular culture in general and TV shows in particular. Interestingly enough, these names are usually not those of the actors and actresses, but of the roles they play.

Many a Jamie owes her identity to the Bionic Woman, but how many of them know that the role was played by actress Lindsay Wagner? Jill, always a fairly popular girls' name, got a big boost from Farrah Fawcett's character in the show *Charlie's Angels*, and no doubt a few Farrahs were also named for the actress. Among boys, some of those named Jason may have actor Robert Brown to thank for their names—or to grump at, in case Jason isn't the name they would like to have. Brown played the role of Jason Bolt in an early TV series *Here Come the Brides*.

Quite a few of today's babies will find out when they're older that their first names came from the characters in the extremely popular daytime serials *General Hospital, All My Children,* and others. Among TV-inspired names are:

Monica	Bobbie	Holly
Alan	Amy	Brian
Leslie	Mike	Claudia
Rick	Jimmy Lee	Jesse
Luke	Celia	Tara
Laura	Grant	Devon

Being a celebrity or well-known person has its problems. TV and movie stars are constantly being asked for their autographs. The written name of a famous person is far more than a hurried scrawl across the page. It connects the awestruck recipient to the celebrity.

A well-known author recently had an autographing workout, even though his audience was invisible. While there weren't six thousand screaming fans demanding Edwards Park's signature, this contributing editor of *Smithsonian* magazine and author of the book *Treasures of the Smithsonian* did have an exhausting but funny experience with his name.

Here is Edwards Park's story as it appeared in the January 1984 *Smithsonian:*

> A couple of months back I gently plugged *Treasures of the Smithsonian,* but I didn't mention that I had to hand-sign 6,000 deluxe, leather-backed, cased copies. This was to fulfill the promise that these expensive editions would be personally autographed. And I wouldn't mention it now, except that Clifton E. Gary of Midwest City, Oklahoma, wrote in complaining because the signature had been printed by a machine, not penned by hand.
>
> Well, sir, you might say that by the time I got through four full days of signing my name I was more a machine than a man, but the fact remains that your book, plus 5,999 others,

was signed by a human hand, gloved and bandaged against blisters, often cramped, always sweaty, barely living, but mine, all mine, nonetheless. I went out to the W. A. Krueger Company printing plant in New Berlin, Wisconsin, sat down at a smooth, clean table, and took on huge stacks of books, layer after layer. It was really quite an experience.

Two delightful ladies, Hilda and Ida, were detailed to help. Hilda shoved a book in front of me, opened to the title page; I signed my name and skidded the volume to Ida who slammed it into its case and stacked it aside. A man with a forklift set the stacks into huge cartons and hauled them away when they were topped off. Going full throttle, we were able, after some experience, to finish a layer of 90 books in about 12 minutes—a rate that I think may qualify for the *Guinness Book of World Records.*

Now, I have to admit that my signature suffered slightly in the process. I took care to make the first signing of a 90-book layer a careful—nay, almost *artistic*—one, but then the rhythm of piecework took over, and I was never really sure what I was writing at that speed. I would try to get off a good "E" and a fine, artistic "P," but what went on in between surpasses the imagination. My mind drifted away during the endless, idiotic repetition. I became Edwards Pink, Pork, Peak, Punk.

"Edwards" also took it heavy. It's a difficult name at best, and crossing the second "d" didn't help it any, "Edwarts." When, on one record-breaking run, I began counting the copies in the layer, I got up to "eleven," and—you guessed it—wrote Eleven Park. I saved it only by tortuous artistry including the addition of that bewildering "s."

Twice I started to reverse my name, "Park Edwards." What the heck, it sounds just as good, and it certainly didn't make any difference to me at that point. I caught it in time to squeeze the first name in before the last. Once I really botched the initial "E." The pen stumbled, and the letter came out looking like a Chinese ideograph. I couldn't fix it, I just let her go and underlined it, defiantly, as if to tell the reader that I *always* sign my name like that. Maybe some-day it will be worth a lot of money, like a stamp with an inverted airplane on it, but I doubt it.

Edwards Park's name is now better known and, after this experience, should be widely respected, especially by the 6,000 owners of his autographed book.

Suppose you happen to have a celebrity's name. Can you become celebrated in your own right? It is unlikely, but here's an exception. Jimmy Carter, thirteen, of Enfield, a Philadelphia suburb, was walking home from school on a winter day when he heard a noise coming from a nearby pond. Realizing that someone had fallen through the thin ice, Jimmy rushed to hail an approaching school bus. The driver, Glen Angus, stopped his bus, plunged into the water, and rescued two girls, five and seven. Without the quick action of Glen Angus and Jimmy Carter, both girls would probably have drowned. The two heroes received citations for bravery from the community.

Young celebrities, especially those in the theater, movies, and television, may have unusual names, but these are often their own. Taking a professional name that looks or sounds better on movie credits or TV screen is not done as much as it used to be. Since unusual names are memorable, young actors who have them often keep them. On the evening TV show *Domestic Life*, Martin Mull's ten-year-old son is played by a boy actor with a hyphenated last name, Christian Brackett-Zika. Ever since he was little, eleven-year-old Rodney Donald Robb, who had a supporting role in the film *A Christmas Story* and also does TV commercials, stage, and film work the year round, has been known by everyone as R. D. Robb.

Suppose you want to be a celebrity and you're not as well known as a Farrah Fawcett, Edwards Park, or R. D. Robb? You could do something to your name, the way Beatles' fan Charles F. Rosenay did. Mr. Rosenay, of New Haven, Connecticut, is editor and publisher of *Good Day Sunshine*, a magazine devoted to the Beatles. He decided he needed to be better known, so, inspired by a Beatles' song chorus, "She loves you, yeah! Yeah! Yeah!", Charles F. Rosenay legally became Charles F. Rosenay!!! Mr.

Rosenay's name now appears everywhere as Rosenay!!!—even on his driver's license.

Suppose you want to be famous and your only attribute is that you are a male who has a jolly personality? What better way could there be than for you to become Santa Claus? At least two men and maybe three have done just that. And it's perfectly legal.

Leroy S. Scholtz of Newton, New Jersey, has spent more than twenty-five years playing Santa Claus throughout the world. He has a Social Security card with the name Santa C. Claus and in 1980 was mentioned in newspapers when he went to court to have the name made legal. He succeeded. In his case, the C stands for Christopher, according to Mr. Scholtz.

Another legal Santa Claus had an original name just a bit closer to the real thing than Leroy Scholtz's. Winfred Eugene Holly of Los Angeles had his name change to Santa Claus approved by the court in 1982. Should he ever have a daughter, he could call her Holly Santa Claus.

The third Santa Claus, middle name also Christopher, lives in the tiny town of North Pole, in the Adirondack Mountains of New York state. His driver's license reads Santa C. Claus, but he says his original name is lost and that he is ageless. (Actually, he was born in Chicago in 1927.) This Santa Claus drives a red and white Thunderbird and is a retired postman who now earns his living by modeling and making personal appearances. He has been playing the part off and on since 1956. Where was he born? What did he do before he became a Santa Claus? Will the real Santa Claus please stand up?

Dan Bloom of Nome, Alaska, is working to make celebrities of two mythical characters named Bubbie and Zadie. These names mean grandmother and grandfather in Yiddish, and Bloom's idea is to give Jewish children someone to write to at Hanukkah, the way other children write Christmas letters to Santa Claus. In just over two years, Bloom's Bubbie and Zadie have received more than 3,000 letters. Bloom has answered every one.

Members of royalty are automatic celebrities, so their names are all-important. It reportedly took a week, and a bit of argument, before Prince Charles and Princess Diana of England chose William as the name for their first son (full name, William Arthur Philip Louis). Since the little prince may one day succeed his father as king of England, the royal family wanted a suitable name, one they hoped would make nicknaming difficult. Shortly after the name was announced, however, one British newspaper dubbed the young heir to the throne Billy the Kid. And Charles himself fell under the spell of nicknaming, dubbing his son Wills. An earlier William of England, William IV, who reigned from 1830 to 1837, had a less endearing nickname. He was called Silly Billy.

Some British royal servants have had hilariously appropriate names. Hurl, a chauffeur, once stopped the royal car so suddenly that the Queen Mother tumbled forward out of the seat. A Coldstream Guard named Footer was punished for stepping on a tourist's foot. There were once royal detectives named Officer and Sharp. And a Mrs. Innocent was Queen Victoria's nurse. To top it off, the farm manager at Windsor Castle was a Mr. Reeks, quite appropriate to barnyard duties, even royal ones.

Part Three

A Name Grab Bag

10 *Interesting and Unusual Names*

We don't laugh at the Smalls, Townes, Greens, and Bakers of this world, even though it may be strange to be identified through size, place, color, or occupation. That's because these are accepted names. But some names attract our attention because they are unexpectedly suitable or funny. We chuckle at Owen Letter at the Flourtown, Pennsylvania, Post Office, or at Miss Apple, who has a fruit store.

Some of the interest and even the humor of names comes from coincidence and some from accidental or intentional but odd couplings of first and last names. Many times, simply the sound of a name makes it unusual and often amusing.

The coincidental category is a large one, composed of names that may or may not be unusual in themselves, but that become interesting and perhaps funny when coupled with an occupation or a situation.

Once upon a time there was a South Carolina law firm with the name of Ketchum & Cheatham! Although the overwhelming majority of attorneys neither catch their clients nor cheat them, the law, like any other profession, is not without its less-than-perfect practitioners. Such a name brings rueful chuckles.

In what was considered a silly survey by some who were questioned, people whose names reflected their occupa-

tions unanimously said they did not undertake those occupations because of their names. Among them were Hugh Law, attorney; Lacy L. Toothman, dentist; Tom Eagle, veterinarian; Donald Stone, geologist; Norman "Brick" Wall, architect; and Jack J. Barber, barber.

We wonder how people feel about the relationship of their names to what they do. Victor Lovely is an alleged terrorist, James Rotton is an air pollution researcher, Lawrence Wrightsman teaches psychology and the law, Hugh Foot edits *Pedestrian Accidents Magazine,* while Mark Leary solves problems related to social anxiety. A member of the U.S. Marine Corps is actually named Michael Marine, and Dr. Ray L. Birdwhistell is an authority on nonverbal communication!

In corporate giant RCA, quite a few people have names related to their work. Lawrence Rockett, for instance, does NASA project research, while Paul Hammer is a machine shop worker. Although it doesn't involve her job, Eileen Wing loves flying. RCA's Charles Seals does not have a

walrus mustache, but his hobby is collecting replicas of his seagoing namesake.

Additional appropriate names include Dr. Susan Luck, a surgeon who depends on skill, and Phyllis Trueluck, who needs all the luck she can get. She spends several hours a day as an underwater lecturer in the shark tank at Sea World, Orlando, Florida. Then there's Storm Field—christened Elliot, but always known by his nickname—son of Frank Field and a second-generation TV weatherman; Paul Officer, who was at one time the chief bodyguard to Princess Diana of the British royal family; and finally Robin Banks, a dedicated employee who works for a bank.

Coincidental names include a Pennsylvania man named Crooks, who was adjudged innocent of a supposed crime, and an Englishman named Innocence, who was found guilty of forging checks.

In the days before modern firearms, early muskets used flint struck against steel to create the spark that ignited the gunpowder and fired the gun. We have to wonder if this bit of history ignited the romance between the now-married Elizabeth Woodbury Flint and Francis Penn Steel, Jr.

The Stoneyhurst Quarries of Bethesda, Maryland, have been selling stone since 1832, and from the first day in business, the quarry has been run by members of the Stone family.

History was made or, rather, reversed in 1979, when President Carter absolved Dr. Samuel Mudd from any role in the 1865 assassination of President Abraham Lincoln. Dr. Mudd was the physician who set assassin John Wilkes Booth's leg, broken in his leap from a box to the stage of Ford's Theater. Dr. Mudd learned about the assassination only after performing his medical services. Imprisoned, the doctor was released after four years by President Andrew Johnson. Although this good Samaritan was pardoned, the Mudd family believed a pardon implied guilt and that Dr. Mudd was due a vote of confidence. It came only after several generations of the Mudd family had been petitioning six Presidents for 114 years! It made a happy man of Dr. Richard Mudd, Dr. Samuel's grandson. And, finally, the news was relayed to the grandson by a distant cousin, then TV anchorman Roger Mudd of CBS. At last the sting was removed from the old saying, "His name is mud."

First- and last-name couplings can be unusual too. Sometimes they are accidental, like Rush Attaway; the first name is an old family name. But this name is considerably easier to live with than such real-life combinations as Zippity Duda, Aquarius Beasley, Unwanted Jones, Asad Experience Wilson, Polly Wogg, and Upson Downs.

Name oddities abound in a family whose last name is Gunn. Their daughter, Betty B., is nicknamed B.B., while brother Thomas goes by Tommy. Mr. Gunn's name is Richard, but everybody calls him Pop.

Odd name combinations are rooted in American history. Among the names reported in the U.S. Census of 1790 were: Sarah Simpers, Ruth Shaves, and Mourning Chestnut.

Letter-only names are as close as people can come to having no last names at all. The Social Security Administration reports twenty-four people named A, four each named B, C, D, E, F, G, H, I, J, K, and L, and at least one person each whose last name is one of the other fourteen letters of the alphabet.

There are occasional number-only names. The strangest one ever recorded by the state of Florida was 5/8 Johnson. Essayist Russell Baker had a childhood friend whose first name was Eleven. He was the eleventh child, and his family just ran out of name ideas.

Moving from short to long, Shantha Jayashekaramurthy at age thirteen won the 1980 Greater Philadelphia spelling bee by correctly spelling "manifestation," easy indeed compared with the spelling of her own name. The family generally shortens its last name to Murthy, but Shantha prefers the full seventeen-letter name.

The longest geographical name in the United States is forty-three-letter Lake Chargoggagoggmanchaugaggog-chaubunagungamaug near Webster, Massachusetts. The lake was the site, in 1983, for a meeting of more than three thousand American Indians representing some fifty tribes. The name means "the boundary fishing place, the neutral meeting grounds." It has been a tribal gathering place for centuries.

Longer by fifteen letters is the Welsh town of Llanfair-pwllgwyngyllgogerychwyrndrobwllllantysiliogogogoch. Its railway station, recently offered for sale, included a nameplate and a pronunciation lesson. In English, the long-handled name means "St. Mary's Church in the hollow of the white hazel [tree] near a rapid whirlpool and the church of St. Tysilio near a red cave." Look again—the name is even longer in English!

Sometimes, names are just plain confusing. Nancy and Louis Piga of Minneapolis wrote a letter to *Time* magazine thanking Miss Piggy of *Muppets* fame for agreeing to pose for the *Mona Piga*. Thanks to Miss Piggy's decision, "our name has become a household word," Mrs. Piga reported.

At last, confusion had ended. No longer was the family name written as Biga, Pica, and Pizza!

Humorists have long used names for getting laughs. A humorist of Abraham Lincoln's time called himself Petroleum V. Nasby. More recently, people enjoyed the comedy of Colonel Lemuel Q. Stoopnagle. Colonel Stoopnagle often made up funny names. Among them: Isaiah Unhh, whose job was trying to open stuck railroad coach windows; and Phoebe B. Beebe, of Saugatuck near Naugatuck, Connecticut.

In pre-TV days, the radio daytime serial *Vic and Sade* used names for humorous effect. Vic and Sade's family name, for instance, was Guck. The show included twins, Robert and Slobbert Hibbert, and a character with the unlovely name of Charlie Razorscum! A better-known radio and movie performer of the time was ventriloquist Edgar Bergen. His brightest dummy was Charlie McCarthy, but his cast of characters also included funny-name dummies Mortimer Snerd and Effie Klinker.

To end this chapter, nothing could be more appropriate than the true story of the man who grew tired of having just another name. Neil McDonagh of Comber, Northern Ireland, had his name changed to Zebedee Zzypp, giving himself, as he said, "the name to end all names." It did, too. It is the last name in his local telephone book.

11 Names
Go Underground

Sometimes, names go underground to protect the people who take them there. Other names are already underground, since they are nicknames and code names that criminals give each other. And while not all nicknames are underground by any means, they often replace the first names of the famous in the eyes of the public.

An underground name can be a better disguise than even the best false whiskers or dyed hair, especially in the shadowy world of international spying (also known by other names: espionage, intelligence, and counterintelligence).

Spies have existed since the biblical days of Samson, the strong man who was betrayed by Delilah, a paid agent of the Philistines. One of the most famous spies of World War I was Mata Hari. She was born in the Netherlands with the original name Margaret Gertrude Macleod. Her mother was Dutch; her father, Scottish. She married a Dutch colonial officer named Zelle, who was stationed in Java, and chose the Malay name Mata Hari, meaning "sun." It was in Java that this unusually beautiful woman learned the dancing skills that would later make her a well-known personality in Europe. This led her into espionage for the Germans and to her eventual capture and execution by the French. Unfortunately for her, Mata Hari was a far better dancer than she was a spy. Legend has given her an

undeserved reputation for espionage. History repeated itself thirty-five years later, in 1952, when Mata Hari's daughter, Banda, was shot as a spy by the Korean Communists.

In World War II, a minor British criminal was captured by the Germans when they invaded the Channel Islands off the British coast. He agreed to spy for the Germans, who arranged to return him secretly to Britain. His mission was to destroy an aircraft factory. The Germans reasoned, wrongly, that the spy would gladly work against the country where he was wanted for safecracking. But the would-be spy, Eddie Chapman, turned himself in and worked for British intelligence instead. As a double agent, pretending to spy for Germany, Chapman plotted with British camouflage experts to make it appear from the air that the aircraft factory had indeed been badly damaged. He reported by secret radio to the Germans that his mission had been accomplished. Chapman sneaked in and out of England several times, continuing to pretend to spy for the Germans while secretly working against them. Unlike many spies, he survived the war. The most interesting part of Chapman's story was his very appropriate nickname. He was called Zig-Zag for his supposed double-agent activities.

Among the code names, not always appropriate, for other famous double agents are the Snark, Mutt and Jeff, Garbo, Biscuit, Careless, Butterfly (*papillon* in French), Sweet William (the name of a flower), the Worm, and Washout. We hope Careless and Washout didn't live up to their code names.

One spy who, like Eddie Chapman, lived to tell the tale is Dusko Popov, the most celebrated double agent of World War II. Known to the British, for whom he spied, as Tricycle, to the Germans, whom he double-crossed, he was simply Ivan.

Popov posed as an admirer of Nazism and became a German spy but actually he forwarded valuable secret information to the British. He risked his life repeatedly, and his exploits are said to have been Ian Fleming's inspiration for the James Bond (Agent 007) spy novels. Among Popov's real-life adventures was relaying advance warning of the bombing of Pearl Harbor to the FBI!

Another way in which names go underground is the federal government's witness protection program. In exchange for their valuable testimony, some witnesses in criminal cases receive light sentences or are acquitted. Because the risk to their lives is so great, the government often gives these witnesses new names and relocates them to new areas where, it is hoped, they will not be found by the criminals against whom they have testified in court.

Not all nicknames hide secrets. Here are labels of a few stage and movie personalities, musicians, sports figures, military leaders, politicians, and gangsters from the 1920s:

Scarface	The Terrible	Babyface
Fatty	Pig Woman	Bugs
Mad Dog	Peaches	Gimpy
Bing	Shoeless Joe	Little Augie
Kid	Pussyfoot	Black Jack
Big Bill	Jake	Babe
Duke	Kingfish	Gurrah
Chick	Machine Gun Jack	Buck

The name Scarface belonged to Al Capone, probably the most feared criminal of his generation. Other Capone nicknames were the Beast, the Behemoth, Big Al, the Big Boy, the Big Fellow, the Big Guy, Al Brown, Tony Scarface, and Snorky.

Roscoe "Fatty" Arbuckle, also gracing this unique list, was a silent film comedian. Singer Harry Lillis "Bing" Crosby, and the commander of the American Expeditionary Force in World War I, General John J. "Black Jack" Pershing received their own indelible stamps—memorable nicknames.

The world of jazz had its royalty, starting before 1920 with trumpeter King Oliver. Later members of the court included Duke Ellington, who liked the nickname, and Count Basie, who didn't. Pianist Earl Hines, however, is not a member of this circle. Earl is his real first name; his nickname is Fatha.

Two men who changed their names played important parts in U.S. history. The first made the change because he was accused of a crime. The second could not change his name in life, but did so in death. Neither man was born in the United States, nor did they die here, and the second man never set foot in the country. Here are their surprising name stories.

In 1772, a twenty-five-year-old Scottish-born captain bought a ship in the West Indies. The next year, he killed the leader of his mutinous crew, an action he later called the "great misfortune" of his life. Instead of standing trial for his crime, he changed his name and fled. Two years later, he surfaced in Virginia, where he received a share of his dead brother's estate. He was commissioned a senior lieutenant in the Continental Navy. Among his many heroic exploits, he is best remembered for his amazing naval victory against the British ships *Serapis* and *Countess of Scarborough* off the Scottish coast. When challenged by the British to surrender, he said, "I have not yet begun to fight." He died in Paris in 1792, but it took more than a hundred years for the United States to bring his body back to his adopted country for the hero's burial he deserved. His grave at Annapolis, Maryland, is a national shrine. History knows him as John Paul Jones. His original name: John Paul.

James Macie was born in France in 1765. Unfortunately for him, his parents were not married and his father did not recognize James as his son. Although his father was a member of the British nobility, his mother failed in her efforts to gain James the recognition he deserved. He was made a naturalized British subject, but he was denied all other rights of a British citizen, including the use of his true family name, because of his unrecognized birth.

Nevertheless, he graduated from college and became a

brilliant and wealthy scientist, all the time harboring resentment against the intractable British government. Not wanting to pass his own recognition problems on to his children, James Macie never married. And when he died in 1829, the inheritor of his great wealth was the United States of America, a place he had never seen.

His gift to this country was very specific: James Macie wanted, and received, the recognition of his father's name the British had denied him. His money was used to create an institution that is today one of the world's largest storehouses of knowledge and historical materials. The Smithsonian Institution, in Washington, D.C., recognizes his rightful family name, Smithson.

12 *High Tech and Your Name*

Exotic-sounding first names were mentioned back in Chapter 6. How about these for newborns: Hero, Elektro, Genus, Scamp, and Shaky? Not exactly easy names to live with, but acceptable because these "people" are robots. Companies producing mechanoids give them unusual names to make them more attractive to the buying public. Heathkit's Hero I is a great success. His chunky figure ambles around as he introduces displays at manufacturing conventions or role-plays as a classroom instruction tool.

Robots like Hero I would be far behind their present state of the art, as scientists call the latest advance, without the modern computer. The computer is the robot's mind. Computers perform mathematical tasks like figuring out a family's electric bill and bank balance or directing remote machinery. But computers can do these things only because they are giant storehouses of information in miniature.

Imagine an office building many stories high, filled with filing cabinets. Imagine each cabinet loaded with files. Now think of one file with your name on it, and little notes inside listing every telephone call you ever made from home. Next, think of a person taking an elevator from the first to the fiftieth floor, walking down a long corridor, entering one of the file rooms, opening a file drawer, finding your file, and entering by hand your last month's phone calls with their costs. This job might take a half hour or longer, but it can be done in a few seconds by a computer, which also makes up your phone bill, with your name, and puts it in the mail. Computers are useful because of the time and work they save.

A computer memory bank replaces this building full of files with tiny chips. Each chip stores lots of information. The computer operator, by pressing a few buttons, can pull your file from thousands of others and, in a second or two, show the information in it on a screen.

Computers need a key to unlock the information in them. That key is someone's name.

How has the computer revolution affected names? For one thing, you, or your parents, get far more third-class mail today than a few years ago. In the last fifteen years, the laborious typing out of addresses to customers, charity donors, and voters has been replaced by computer quickness, which results in much so-called junk mail. You and your name are now highlighted, for better or worse, thanks to high tech.

One reason your mailbox is so full is that computerized mailing lists grow. This happens because one company that adds your name to its list often sells that list to other mail-order companies. Reply to one letter from an environmental group, for instance, and your mailbox will soon be filled with mail from others.

Recently, a woman wrote to a newspaper advice columnist asking how she could get mail. The reply was, "Buy something—anything—by mail. You'll soon have all the catalogs and letters you could want."

Computers use something besides your name, or your parents' name, to reach you with mail. Their operators also use those five special numbers, your zip code. The people who market everything by mail, from pickled herring to politicians, know that people often respond to certain kinds of mail depending on where they live. Some direct-

mail experts have divided zip codes into many categories, from superwealthy to very poor, from inner city to near-wilderness. They use these categories to target mailings to people who can be expected to welcome them. Everyone in a certain affluent zip code category might be mailed gourmet food catalogs, but a mailing about chain saws and log splitters would be targeted to wooded zip code areas only.

"You are where you live" is the way one direct-mail expert puts it. If your zip code shows that you and your neighbors are more likely to be Democrats than Republicans, or the other way around, your family can count on getting more fund-raising letters from representatives, senators, and presidential candidates of the party that has the voting edge in your area than from the opposition. If you or your family have ever sent money to a political party or a charity organization, you're considered "mail-responsive" and will receive many more requests for money—all thanks to computers.

Surely you've had mail come to your house addressed to Occupant. Some senders blanket a neighborhood by occupant, because such mailing lists cost less than by-name lists. If you buy from an occupant catalog, you also become mail-responsive; that is, by adding your name to the catalog reply coupon, you become part of another name list. Since computers can handshake or interface with one another, your name is added to different lists automatically, computer-to-computer instead of person-to-person.

Once they have your name in their data banks, computers have another way of singling you out. They help companies to personalize messages by printing your name throughout a form letter. For example:

> Dear Mr. Accetta:
> You have been chosen by The Door Prize Company to receive one of our many valuable prizes. This is your lucky day, Mr. Accetta. Be sure to call us at 1-212-486-7136 to claim your prize. We will look forward to your call, Mr. Accetta, and will send your prize to 517 Cornelia Place.
> Sincerely,
> The Door Prize Company

Sometimes the computer will capitalize the MR. AC-CETTA parts of such letters, to remind you that you are being personally addressed. Usually, such "prizes" are offered in connection with some kind of purchase, proving the truth of the old saying, "There's no such thing as a free lunch."

You can see by this example that the computer makes both you and your name accessible.

How can computers insert thousands of personal names, and often their addresses or cities, in form letters? They do it by working with high-speed printing equipment to include your name, along with special numbers in mail advertising sweepstakes and other contests. As in the letter above, your name appears to have been printed just for you, and the personalized parts match the printed areas almost perfectly.

Since a computer can't think but only gives back the information a person programs into it, funny name mistakes can and do happen. Suppose your name is Lee S. Richards, Jr., and the computer programmer's attention wanders for a moment when your name is entered into the system. You might get a computer letter beginning "Dear Mr. Jr." instead of "Dear Mr. Richards." Or your school has sent for equipment. The next letter comes back, "Dear Mr. School."

Sometimes computers aren't programmed with complete names. The authors' daughter, Barbara, was listed as Barba on just one computer list. Now, she gets Barba Lee mail from several sources.

Another way in which high tech uses your name is in records and forms. The secretary in your doctor's office may use a computer keyboard to print information onto a form. If your parents have medical insurance, a lot of time is saved for the doctor, your dad, and the insurance companies when computers help with paperwork. As with other computer-generated forms, the numbers are important, but your name is the key.

The day may come when computers know all about you, once they are given your name and Social Security number. Even now, they know a lot. If your parents should go to a bank to borrow money to buy a car or make improvements to your home, they fill out a long form that tells about their ability to repay the loan. How long does it take the bank to respond? Almost no time at all. By phone, the bank people ask the credit bureau in or near your parents' town to compare its computer information about your family's credit history with the information on the loan application. Although the bank makes the final decision about granting the loan, the fact that information can be retrieved, or taken out, of the credit bureau's computer in seconds lets the bank make its decision quickly. One bank in Philadelphia advertises same-day loan approvals, provided the loan request reaches the bank by 10 A.M.

Computers may be homing in on our names, but they will never be our names. What a strange statement. Yet, think about it: Names were once chosen for persons, places and *things*. People named themselves after a tree, a fruit, a hill, river, brook, or house. If we were still choosing names, might we not be Sally Computer, Jonathan Byte, or Carlos Robot?

Perhaps it's just as well that our names are already fixed in history. They give us a good balance in the fast-changing world of high technology and remain constant in a society ever on the move.

Dictionary
of Common Last Names
and Their Meanings

There are 1,286,556 different surnames in the United States. It would take many books to include them all. Here are the most popular names; many include different nationalities.

The numbers after fifty of the names indicate where they stand in popularity in the United States according to a recent survey. For example, Adams is the 38th most common name in the United States.

ADAMS (38), ADAMSON, ADDAMS: son of Adam, red earth

ADLER: eagle *(German)*

ALLEN (25), ALLAN, ALAN: descendant of Alan, handsome or harmonious

ANDERSON (9), ANDERSEN, ANDREWS, ANDERS: son of Andrew, strong, manly

BA: three; grandmother; poison residue *(Vietnamese)*

BACINO: little kiss *(Italian)*

BAKER (33): maker of bread

BAKESTER, BAXTER: a lady baker or a baker's wife

BARBARO, BARBERINI, BARBERINO: foreigner *(Italian)*

BARON: bat arm; son of Aaron, exalted one

BERKOWITZ: son of Berko *(Polish)*

BERNSTEIN: dealer in amber *(German)*

BOCCA: mouth *(Italian)*

BOCCACCIO: ugly mouth *(Italian)*

BONGIOVANNI: good John *(Italian)*

BIANCHI, BIANCO: one with white hair or a light complexion *(Italian)*

BROWN (4), BROUN, BROWNE: dark-skinned

BRUNI: one with a dark, or brown, complexion *(Italian)*

CAMPANA, CAMPANELLI, CAMPANELLA, CAMPANELLO: bell *(Italian)*

CAMPBELL: (41) a person with raised or arched lips

CAPRA: goat *(Italian)*

CARTER (43): one who transports objects in a cart

CASTRO: fort, from the Latin *castrum (Spanish)*

CHI: lead; mind; show; elder sister *(Vietnamese)*

CHIANG: river *(Chinese)*

CH'IEN: money *(Chinese)*

CLARK (18), CLARKE, CLERK: someone who reads and writes

COHEN: of priestly lineage *(Hebrew)*

COLLINS (48), COLLINGS, COLLIN, COLIN: from nickname for Nicholas, victory of the people

COLÓN *(Spanish)*; COLUMBO *(Italian)*; COLUMBUS: dove or pigeon

CRUZ: symbol of the cross *(Spanish)*

DAVIS (7), DAVIES, DAVISON, DAVIDSON: son of Davie or David, friend

DE ANGELIS, DE ANGELI, DE ANGELO, D'ANGELO: son of Angelo *(Italian)*

DE MARCHI: son of Marchi *(Italian)*

106

DE MARCO, DI MARCO: son of Marco, who belongs to Mars *(Italian)*

DE SANTIS *(Portuguese)*; DE SANTO, DI SANTO, DI SANTI *(Italian)*: son of Sante, the saint

DÍAZ: son of Diago, or Diego, from the Hebrew Jacob, which means supplanter *(Spanish)*

DONG: copper; a pile; more *(Vietnamese)*

EDELMAN: noble man; husband of Edel, or Adele *(German)*

EDOGAWA: near the river *(Japanese)*

EDWARDS (50): son of Edward, a guardian of property

ESPÓSITO: exposed (Italian mothers who could not keep their newborn would leave them at a convent door, where the sisters would raise them, naming them Espósito)

EVANS (45), EVANSON: son of Evan, Welsh form of John

FERNÁNDEZ: son of Fernando, which means journey *(Spanish)*

FINKELSTEIN: Yiddish for pyrites, a mineral associated in folklore with good fortune *(German)*

FIORE, FIORI: one who lives near flowers *(Italian)*

FRIEDMAN: peaceful person *(German)*

FULLER: one who thickens cloth by adding particles called fuller's earth

GAMBA, GAMBINO, GAMBINI, GAMBETTA, GAMBONE: leg *(Italian)*

GARCÍA (44): Gerald *(Spanish)*

GATTO, GATTI, GATTINO: cat *(Italian)*

GIGLIO, GIGLI: one who lives near lilies *(Italian)*

GINSBERG, GINSBURG: from Gunzburg, a Bavarian town

GOLDBERG: gold mountain, from several such places; a name chosen by many Jewish families expelled from Siberia *(German)*

GÓMEZ: son of Gomo, nickname for Gomesano, famous warrior *(Spanish)*

GONZALEZ (42), GONZALES: son of Gonzalo, the young warrior *(Spanish)*

GREEN (37), GREENE: dweller near a grassy field

GUERRA, GUERRINA, GUERRERO: war or warrior *(Spanish)*

GUTIÉRREZ: son of Gutierre, a form of Walter, made from the German words for rule and folk *(Spanish)*

HALL (24): the person in charge of a castle or manor; from the great hall, the center of castle life

HARADA: field, plow *(Japanese)*

HARRISON (11), HARRIS, HARRIES: son of Harry, a ruler

HERNÁNDEZ: son of Hernando, a form of Fernández *(Spanish)*

HILL (32), HILLS, HILLMAN: someone who lives on or near a rise of ground

HONG: flank or side; red; rosy *(Vietnamese)*

HORWITZ, HOROWITZ: from Horovice, a town in Bohemia *(Russian)*

HSIUNG: bear *(Chinese)*

HUANG: yellow *(Chinese)*

JACKSON (17): son of Jack, a pet name for John, the Lord is gracious

JOHNSON (2), JONSON: son of John, the Lord is gracious

JOHNSTON, JOHNSTONE: from John's manor

JONES (5; *Welsh*); JONAS *(Lithuanian)*: son of John

KAO: high *(Chinese)*

KATZ: from two words meaning priest of righteousness *(Hebrew)*

KHIEM: humble; to need *(Vietnamese)*

KING (28): an entertainer who played royal roles

KY: to sign; strange; abstain from; to rear; carefully *(Vietnamese)*

LAN: blue *(Chinese)*

LEE (35), LEA, LEY, LEIGH: someone living in or near a pasture or meadow *(English)*

LEE: walnut tree *(Korean)*

LEI: thunder *(Chinese)*

LEVI, LEVY: descendant of Levi, which means united *(Hebrew)*

LEWIS (20), LEWES: loudest in battle

LI: plum tree; politeness *(Chinese)*

LOEB: lion *(German)*

LUNG: dragon *(Chinese)*

MALASPINA, MALESPINI, MALASPINI: bad thorn *(Italian)*

MAO: hair *(Chinese)*

MARTÍNEZ (8), MARTINSON: Martin's son; from the Latin Martinus, belonging to the god Mars *(Spanish)*

MATSUMOTO: root of pine tree *(Japanese)*

MEDINA: Arabic for market *(Spanish)*

MILLER (6), MILNER, MILLAR: operator of a mill, such as one grinding flour from grain

MINH: the body *(Vietnamese)*

MITCHELL (39), MITCHEL: descendant of Michael, "Who is like God?"

MOORE (13), MOOR, MORE: dweller near or in a marsh

MORALES: son of Moral *(Spanish)*

MORENO, MORO: Moorish; not to be confused with MORA, meaning mulberry *(Spanish)*

MORRIS (27): from Norman-French Maurice, Moorish, dark-skinned

MORRISON, MORISON: Maurice's son

MURATA: village rice field *(Japanese)*

NAKAMURA: middle of the village *(Japanese)*

NAKAYAMA: middle of the mountain *(Japanese)*

NELSON (30), NILSON, NELSEN: son of Nils, a champion *(Scandinavian)*

NEGRI: dark-complexioned; an African *(Italian)*

OGAWA: small river *(Japanese)*

ORTIZ: son of one who is fortunate; from the Latin *fortuna*, fate or success *(Spanish)*

PARKER (49), PARKMAN: a protector of nobles' lands; a game-keeper

PASSARO, PASSAROTTO, PASSEROTTI: sparrow *(Italian)*

PÉREZ: descended from Pero, a nickname for Peter *(Spanish)*

PETERSON (23), PETERSEN, PETERS: son of Peter, a rock

PHAM: greedy; to commit *(Vietnamese)*

PHILLIPS (40), PHILIPS, PHILLIP: son of Philip, one who loves horses

REYES: from the Latin *rex* or *regis*, king *(Spanish); see also* KING

RICHARDS (34), RICHARDSON: son of Richard, strong ruler

RIVERA: one who lives near a river *(Spanish)*

ROBERTS (19), ROBERTSON, ROBERT, ROBART, ROBARD: son of Robert, bright

ROBINSON (22), ROBISON, ROBESON: son of Robin, of shining fame

RODRIGUEZ (31): son of Rodrigo, famous, a ruler *(Spanish)*

ROMA: someone from Rome, four crossroads *(Italian)*

ROSA, ROSSELLI: one who grows or lives near roses *(Italian)*

110

ROSSI, ROSSINI, RUSSO: someone with red hair or a ruddy complexion *(Italian)*

SAKAYA: seller of rice wine *(Japanese)*

SÁNCHEZ: son of Sancho, meaning holy or saintly *(Spanish)*

SANTIAGO: from Saint James, or Jacob, patron saint of Spain *(Spanish)*

SASSO: someone who lives near a rock or a stone *(Italian)*

SCOTT (36): one whose home was Scotland

SHIMADA: island rice field *(Japanese)*

SMITH (1), SMYTHE: one who works with metal

SOLDATO: soldier *(Italian)*

STEWART (47), STEWARD: person in charge of a large household

SUZUKI: wood *(Japanese)*

TAKAHASHI: high bridge *(Japanese)*

TANAKA: middle of the rice field *(Japanese)*

T'ANG: maker of soup *(Chinese)*

TAYLOR (12), TAYLER: tailor, garment maker

TERRANOVA: someone on or from new land *(Italian)*

THIEN: heaven; to geld; expect; narrow-minded *(Vietnamese)*

THIEU: be short; be missing; the minority *(Vietnamese)*

THO: poem; fiber; to breathe; workman *(Vietnamese)*

THOMAS (14), THOMPSON (16): son of Thomas, a twin

TORRE, TORRES: from the Latin *turris*, for watchtower, built by villagers to guard against attack *(Spanish)*

TRAN: to overflow; forehead *(Vietnamese)*

TURNER (46): a worker who turned wood on a lathe

VAN: literature; short-striped tiger; to twist *(Vietnamese)*

111

VASQUEZ: one from the Basque provinces *(Spanish)*

VERDI: one wearing green or living in a green place *(Italian)*

VILLA, VILLANI, VILLARI: resident of a town or country place *(Italian)*

VOLPE, VOLPI: foxy, cunning *(Italian)*

WAGNER (21): wagon maker or driver *(German)*

WALKER (21): one who treats cloth by walking on it

WAN: million *(Chinese)*

WEIN, WEINER, WEINBAUM, WEINBERG: names related to vineyards, wine making, and dealing in wines *(German)*

WHITE (15): from "whiter," a whitewasher of buildings or, more likely, from pale skin

WILLIAMS (3), WILLIAMSON: son of William, a protector

WILSON (10), WILLSON: son of Will, nickname for William

WRIGHT (29): a worker in wood, a carpenter

WRIGHTSON: son of a wright

YAMAMOTO: foot of a mountain *(Japanese)*

YEH: leave *(Chinese)*

YOUNG (26), YOUNGER: used by someone with the same first name as an older person, especially a parent

ZUCKERMAN: dealer in sugar: a candy maker or pastry cook *(German)*

Bibliography

BOOKS

Adamic, Louis. *What's Your Name?* Harper & Brothers, 1942.

Blockson, Charles L., and Ron Fry. *Black Genealogy*. Prentice-Hall, 1977.

Dolan, J. R. *English Ancestral Names: The Evolution of the Surname from Medieval Occupations*. Clarkson N. Potter, 1972.

Gilfond, Henry. *Genealogy: How to Find Your Roots*. Franklin Watts, 1978.

Hilton, Suzanne. *Who Do You Think You Are? Digging for Your Family Roots*. Westminster Press, 1976.

Hilts, Len. *How to Find Your Own Roots*. Greatlakes Living Press, 1977.

Hook, J. N. *Family Names: How Our Surnames Came to America*. Macmillan Publishing Co., 1982.

Kaganoff, Benzion. *A Dictionary of Jewish Names and Their History*. Schocken Books, 1977.

Lee, Mary Price. *Your Name—All About It*. Westminster Press, 1980.

McCormick, Donald. *The Master Book of Spies*. Franklin Watts, 1974.

Pine, L. G. *The Story of Surnames*. Charles E. Tuttle Co., 1966.

ARTICLES

Burzen, Michelle. "How to Trace Your Family Tree," *Ebony*, June 1977, p. 52.

Carlson, Judy. "Is Your Name Right for You?" *Seventeen*, December 1981, p. 104.

"Changing Your Name When You Marry," *Glamour*, September 1979, p. 33.

Walker, Sheila. "What's In a Name? Black Awareness Keeps the African Tradition of 'Meaningful Names' Alive," *Ebony*, June 1977, p. 74.

Acknowledgments

We thank

Ginny Day, again, and her Germantown Academy students for making their past a part of our present book.

Thom Leibowitz of the Elkins Park (Pennsylvania) Middle School.

Bitsy Large, who said, "I would be delighted to have you use my name, inside out, upside down, or any way you choose."

The Rev. Byung Kyu Lee of the Korean Presbyterian Church of Greater Philadelphia.

Rodolfo Rossi, the engaging young plastic surgeon, who may one day join America's roster of new citizens.

Shu Mei Tao of the Dragon Lady Restaurant, Cape May, New Jersey, who happily answered our request for Chinese surnames.

Dick McCarty, Associate Professor of Spanish, Philadelphia Community College, for providing popular Spanish (and German) last names.

Domenica Ascanio DiMarco, Ph.D., Language Laboratory, LaSalle University, Philadelphia.

Margot North, Administrative Assistant to the Editor, *Smithsonian* magazine, who persuaded contributing editor Edwards Park to sign his name yet one more time—on a permission letter for his delightful autographing story.

And, of course,

Fran Accetta, who says she can read the authors' writing and *still* look us straight in the eye.

Finally, our children,

Richard, Barbara, and Monica, *all* of whom changed their names (or nicknames) to those they were more comfortable with . . .

The Lees (the "From the Meadow" people)

Index

118

About the Authors

Mary Price Lee liked to write stories when she was a young girl. Little did she know then that writing would be her lifelong occupation and greatest pleasure. Besides writing, Mrs. Lee enjoys travel, reading, her family—and talking to people about their names.

Richard S. Lee has spent his working life in advertising, as a copywriter, interviewer/photographer, sales promotion coordinator, and creative director. He has written newspaper travel articles and, with Mary Price Lee, high school career books.